FAMILY CHILD CARE

Marketing Guide Second Edition

Being a Family Child Care Professional

Family child care is a special profession for those who love young children. As a professional family child care provider, you must balance the skills required to care for children with those required to operate your business. Here are some tips to help you do this:

- Learn the child care regulations for your area and follow them.
- Join your local family child care association.
- Sign up with your local child care resource and referral (CCR&R) agency.
- Join the Child and Adult Care Food Program (CACFP).
- Find good professional advisers (such as a tax preparer, insurance agent, and lawyer).
- Actively participate in training to acquire and improve your professional skills.

Additional Resources

Redleaf Press and Think Small are two leading national organizations that share the goal of helping your family child care business succeed. Think Small (www.thinksmall .org) can answer your business questions; its website is filled with free handouts and articles. Redleaf Press (www.redleafpress.org; 800-423-8309) publishes resources for family child care. We offer the following publications to support your business:

- Starting a family child care business:
  Family Child Care Business Planning Guide
- Promoting your business:
  Family Child Care Marketing Guide, second edition
- Creating contracts and policies:
  Family Child Care Contracts and Policies, third edition
  Redleaf Complete Forms Kit for Family Child Care Professionals
- Keeping accurate records and filing your taxes:
  Family Child Care Record-Keeping Guide, eighth edition
  The Redleaf Calendar-Keeper: A Record-Keeping System for Family Child Care Professionals
  Family Child Care Tax Workbook and Organizer
  Family Child Care Tax Companion
- Reducing business risks:
  Family Child Care Legal and Insurance Guide
- Managing your money and planning for retirement:
  Family Child Care Money Management and Retirement Guide

All publications (except the *Redleaf Calendar-Keeper* and the *Redleaf Complete Forms Kit for Family Child Care Professionals*) are by Tom Copeland, JD.

DATE	NAME

FAM

M

G

TO

Redleaf
www.redleafpr
800-423-8309

Published by Redleaf Press
10 Yorkton Court
St. Paul, MN 55117
www.redleafpress.org

First edition published 1999. Second edition 2012.
Cover design by Jim Handrigan
Cover photograph © i love images/Veer
Interior design by Erin Kirk New
Typeset in Adobe Garamond Pro and Gill Sans
Printed in the United States of America
19 18 17 16 15 14 13 12   1 2 3 4 5 6 7 8

Library of Congress Cataloging-in-Publication Data
Copeland, Tom.
    Family child care marketing guide / Tom Copeland. — 2nd ed.
      p. cm.
    ISBN 978-1-60554-112-9 (alk. paper)
    1. Family day care—United States—Marketing. 2. Child care services—United
States—Marketing.   I. Title.
    HQ778.63.C66 2012
    362.70973—dc23

Printed on acid-free paper

Contents

CHAPTER EIGHT   How Other Organizations Can Help 113

Appendixes

Acknowledgments

Thanks to the following people for providing valuable feedback and suggestions for this book: Joe Perreault, family child care advocate; Robert Sullivan, Loudoun County Department of Social Services; Sue and Warren Schmidt, Monday Morning America, Inc.; Gershia Coggs, Data Base Inc.; Sue Molstad, Resources for Child Caring; Gail Birch, Provider's Choice Food Program; Diane Phillippi, Ramsey County Family Day Care Licensing Unit; Denise Lane-Porter, Building Blocks Tax Service; Thorton Lam, Child Nutrition, Inc.; Andrea Howlett, Crystal Stairs Food Program; Beverly C. Samuel, Virginia Cooperative Extension; family child care providers Nora Laagard, Grace Emery, Sandy Governor, Beth Mork, Adela Rojas, Lynn Manfredi-Petitt, Peggy Haack; and Reva Wywadis, regional representative of the National Association for Family Child Care. For the first edition of this book, thanks to Redleaf Press team: Dan Verdick, Alyn Bedford, Anne Holzman, Paul Woods, Eileen Nelson, Susan Firestone, and Teina Rowell, and to illustrator Melissa Muldoon. For the second edition, thanks to the Redleaf Press team: David Heath, Kyra Ostendorf, Carla Valadez, and Jim Handrigan.

CHAPTER 1

Introduction to Family Child Care Marketing

The Profession of Family Child Care

Family child care is a unique profession that requires a wide variety of skills: teaching, cooking, mediating, chauffeuring, bookkeeping, organizing, and much, much more. It is a job that hundreds of thousands of women and men perform because they love children and want to support their own families. A family child care professional is not a babysitter. A babysitter is someone who watches children (usually from just one family) for a few hours in the evening while the parents are away from home at a movie or social event. A professional family child care provider is someone who is in the business of teaching and nurturing young children to reach their highest potential, often for more than fifty hours a week year-round. A provider is intentional about planning activities to meet the individual and changing needs of the children in care. This is not an easy job.

At its heart, family child care is about the very personal relationship between a caregiver, a child, and the child's family. This home-centered, personal relationship is what makes family child care so special. At the same time, providers must care for their own physical and emotional needs in order to continue to offer this important service. In the long run, providers must learn to balance the personal and business sides of their profession to be successful.

Being a family child care professional means being in control of your business. You are responsible for setting your own rates and hours, deciding who your customers will be, and choosing what type of curriculum you will offer. Before you care for your first child, you should decide what kind of business you want to have. This is one of the best parts of being self-employed. You are the boss! You are free to set your own rules (as long as they don't violate antidiscrimination laws) and change them whenever you want. Because of this, you should make choices that will make you happy. It doesn't make sense to set up your business, successfully market it to customers, and then quit a year later because you are unhappy with your income or the fact that you didn't have a paid vacation. If you have been in business for a few years and haven't thought carefully about what you want, it is never too late to do so. Once you have defined what you want for your business, marketing becomes a very powerful ally. If you are not in control of your business, marketing it will not make things better. See the *Family Child Care Business Planning Guide* for more information on how to put your business on a solid footing.

This book focuses on family child care marketing. Although I use business terminology when discussing marketing concepts—referring to "finder's fees," "promotions," and "competition," for example—you should understand that offering a high-quality home-based program and marketing it as a business are not contradictory actions. In fact, a comprehensive national study about the quality of family child care concluded that providers are more likely to rank higher on objective measures of quality if they follow standard business practices and charge higher rates! (See *The Study of Children in Family Child Care and Relative Care*, cited in appendix M.)

Being a successful marketer of your business does not mean you must adopt negative business trappings, such as cutthroat competition, high-pressure sales tactics, profit worship, or a win-lose mentality. All providers can achieve success in marketing their business while keeping the casual, homey, friendly, warm, and professional aspects of their program.

For some providers, marketing presents special challenges. We live in a society where discrimination based on race, sex, religion, class, disability, sexual orientation, and ethnic background still exists. In addition, limited educational background or a lack of support agencies and community services can sometimes, but not always, create barriers to success for providers. This book does not attempt to answer how providers can overcome these barriers of discrimination and opportunity, but all family child care providers can improve the amount of pride and control they have in running their own business by following some of the ideas it contains.

What Is Family Child Care Marketing?

Simply stated, family child care marketing is the ongoing communication about your program's benefits to your marketing audience:

- parents who might use your services
- parents who are currently using your services
- parents who formerly used your services

The goal of marketing is to reach parents and compel them to purchase your services. To do this, you need to focus on meeting the needs of both parents and their children. Parents want a safety-conscious, well-trained provider who offers a positive learning environment and learning activities for their children. This book will help you keep the needs of parents and children foremost in your mind.

Many providers think about marketing only when they have an opening to fill. Marketing is not something to do only when you're starting your business or when you have an opening. It is not something to stop once you have a waiting list, because one or more families could leave your program without notice. Successful marketing is about keeping your current clients happy and offering the kind of care your future clients will want. You should be conducting some type of marketing activity every month you are in business.

Marketing your child care program is a never-ending process. As time passes, the needs of parents change. Thirty years ago, few parents sought care for their infants because they stayed home to care for them. Today infant care is in great demand because of the tremendous increase in single-parent and dual-career families. Try to keep up with changing needs in the child care field so your program will be successful in the future. This means asking individuals and organizations a lot of questions about what can help you market your program. For a discussion of how to work with organizations and individuals such as child care resource and referral (CCR&R) agencies, child care regulators, competitors, and employers, see chapter 8.

Marketing and the Quality of Child Care

Operating a high-quality child care program is the foundation of all your marketing efforts. You may be able to attract parents to your program through your promotional efforts, but without a quality program, you won't be able to keep them. Many family child care providers go out of business each year, in large part because they aren't offering high-quality care. Always keep in mind that what you are marketing is your high-quality program, not your house, backyard, or computer. A high-quality program means having child-centered activities, nutritious meals, individual care, and a safe, homey environment run by a trained caregiver. Part of your marketing job is to educate parents about what high-quality child care looks like. Chapter 2 describes how to identify and communicate the benefits of your program so parents will understand why they should enroll their child with you. See appendix E, "Skills Children Learn in Family Child Care," for another helpful resource.

Maintaining a high-quality program also means paying attention to your work environment and identifying what you need to run a stable business that offers consistent care to children. Work-environment issues include income, paid vacations, holidays, sick days, backup help, regular professional-development training, written contracts and policies, and more. See *Family Child Care Contracts and Policies* for details on how to improve your work environment.

About This Book

This book contains a wealth of marketing tips and suggestions, but not all family child care providers have the same needs. If you are just starting out, you may need to fill four to six openings, whereas if you have been in business awhile, you probably need to fill only one or two openings at a time. You do not need to try all of the marketing ideas in this book or make extraordinary efforts at marketing. If you are looking to fill one opening, start small. See "Top Ten Low-Cost Marketing Tips and Estimated Costs" on page 173 for some examples. Many providers gain new clients solely through word-of-mouth recommendations from current clients (see chapter 4). Other providers need to spend much more time and money on marketing and will want to use more of the ideas in this book. Some of the marketing ideas presented here may be best carried out by family child care associations and other support networks. You may want to present some of these ideas to your local organizations for them to implement on behalf of their members. This book is meant to be used selectively over a long period of time.

This book can help you whether you are just starting or have many years of experience. It discusses how to market to prospective clients (chapter 3), current clients (chapter 4), and past clients (chapter 5). It includes many ideas about how to promote your program whether you have a little money or a lot of money (chapter 6). This edition of the book contains a new chapter on how to market using the Internet (chapter 7). You will find information about key organizations that can help you market your family child care program (chapter 8) and a discussion of how to set your rates (chapter 9). This book also answers questions about how to compete against a fancy new child care center as well as unregulated providers (chapter 10). Finally, the appendixes contain sample forms and checklists you can use as part of your marketing program.

Not every idea in this book will appeal to every provider. I encourage you to think carefully about how much marketing is necessary for your business. I do not encourage you to adopt dozens of new marketing tips at the expense of spending less time caring for children. Not every idea will work in your community. Sometimes the same marketing idea that failed this year will succeed next year. This book does not offer an in-depth marketing plan for your business, but it will give you practical tools for developing your own marketing plan based on your own needs. Marketing does not involve science as much as it involves common sense that everyone can apply. The lists of ideas in this book may seem overwhelming at first glance. While I do not expect you to follow every idea presented in this book, I hope you will be open to trying something new. After trying out several ideas, evaluate their impact so you can refocus your next marketing effort (see chapter 11). To help you sort through all the ideas in this book, see appendix A, "Annual Marketing Calendar," which can help you plan your marketing efforts over an entire year.

Throughout this book I often use the words "customer" and "client" to describe the parents who use your services. Some providers are uncomfortable using these terms in their business, but for the purposes of this guide, I will use them to help keep the focus on parent needs. I am not suggesting that all providers must market their program in the same way—far from it! It is up to you to run your business however you want; follow the suggestions in this book that make the most sense to you and your program. The time to start marketing your program is now. You may find out that it can also be fun!

Getting Started in Marketing as a New Provider

What if you are a new family child care provider and know absolutely nothing about how to market your family child care business? How will you begin? Here are the first five steps you should probably take:

1   Find out what parents want from their child care provider. Talk to parents who are using child care now or are looking for child care. Call your local CCR&R agency and talk to a counselor about what parents are looking for in child care programs in your area.

2   Learn from your competition. Contact local child care centers and other family child care providers about their program, curriculum, and any special services they offer parents. Join your local family child care association to connect with other providers. Identify the best providers in your area, and meet with them to learn how they became successful. Ask a provider to be your mentor. Volunteer to work in another provider's home for a few days. Ask your child care licensor and Food Program representative about what other providers offer to parents.

3   Identify the benefits of your program. What do you and your program offer parents and children that would make them want to enroll in your program? Prepare a list of three or four benefits and start communicating them to prospective parents. Include the benefits on your flyers, website, business cards, newsletters, e-mail signature, Craigslist ads, and so on.

4   Set your rates. Get rate information from your local CCR&R agency. Collect rate information by visiting local child care centers and looking at rates posted by other child care programs on the Internet. You cannot discuss rates directly with a competitor, but if the other person doesn't know that you are a family child care provider, you can ask about their rates. See

page 170 for further information about when it's appropriate and legal to talk to other child care programs about their rates.

5   Pick two or three marketing activities from this book and start promoting your program! Prepare an annual calendar and schedule one or two activities each month. Share your results (both positive and negative) with other providers, and then try out new ideas.

I hope that this book will help you take these steps for your new business. Whether you are just starting out or have been in business for many years, this book should take you a long way toward filling spaces in your program.

Book Updates

Chapter 7 contains many links to websites where you can find information to help you promote your business. Because website content tends to change frequently, some of the links may be out of date by the time you read this book. Therefore, I have created a page on my blog (www.tomcopelandblog.com/family-child-care -marketing-guide.html) where I will post updated links to the Internet resources mentioned in this book. On a regular basis, you will also find articles about new marketing ideas on my blog. If you have any ideas you would like to share or suggestions for where to find other marketing information, please let me know. Contact me at tomcopeland@live.com.

Tax Tips

The costs of all marketing ideas listed in this book are tax-deductible expenses for your business. This includes the cost of the following:

- putting up a sign in your front yard
- paying for an online classified ad
- taking pictures of the children in your care
- purchasing business cards
- buying an answering machine or subscribing to a voice mail service
- and much more

This book identifies over a hundred business expenses. Keep the receipt for any item you buy to help market your business. Such marketing expenses should be entered on your IRS **Schedule C Profit or Loss from Business**, on the line for advertising expenses. You can claim these deductions if you are a regulated provider or are exempt from regulations. For more information about what you can deduct as a business expense, see the *Family Child Care Record-Keeping Guide*, published by Redleaf Press, www.redleafpress.org.

CHAPTER 2

Identifying the Benefits of Your Program

Future Trends in the Child Care Field

The child care field has experienced tremendous change in the last thirty years, and it will likely undergo significant changes in the future. What are some trends providers might expect to see? Although largely a matter of guesswork, here are some possible trends that may affect your program:

- Competition from other child care programs will continue to increase. There will be more regulated family child care homes, child care centers, nursery schools, employer-sponsored centers, school-age programs, and preschools, among other competitors.

- Competition from providers who are exempt from state regulations will increase. These providers tend to charge lower fees.

- Competition from large child care centers will increase. These centers—often a part of larger corporations or for-profit chains—will have money to spend on mass-media advertising and expensive facilities.

- With expanded child care choices, parents will demand more and more from their caregivers, such as longer hours, more flexible schedules, more individual attention for their child, or access to the newest technologies. If one program won't meet their needs, parents will be more likely to leave and enroll in another program.

- Providers will notice a greater demand for more specialized child care services: sick care, drop-in care, weekend and evening care, and care for children with a wide range of physical and mental abilities. It will become harder and harder to operate a program that serves only preschoolers, Monday through Friday, from 7:00 a.m. to 6:00 p.m.

- As competition grows, more child care programs will close down because of financial pressures. Most family child care providers operate with a very small profit. With few expenses to cut, any loss of enrollment will quickly create a financial emergency. Providers will have to learn how to plan for the ups and downs of enrollment.

- Child care openings will take longer to fill. This means providers will have to spend more time and money on advertising and promoting their program.

- Child care providers that have good business skills and the ability to communicate with parents will be more likely to succeed.

- Although the overall demand for child care will continue to grow slowly, the greatest growth in the population of children under the age of six will be from nonwhite children.

- More children in child care will be from single-parent households.

- The number of family child care associations, networks, and support groups will increase. Providers who are not a part of these groups will find it more difficult to be visible to potential customers.

- With an increasing number of states offering Quality Rating Improvement Systems (QRIS) (see page 48), more parents will look for objective standards of quality when choosing a child care program. They will want programs that can demonstrate that they are educationally sound.

- The percentage of children enrolled in regulated family child care homes will continue to decline. This percentage has been on the decline for a number of years. This trend will likely continue unless child care providers use the power of marketing to promote their profession.

How can you compete in this competitive environment of the future? When professionals in other industries experience increased competition, they try to lower expenses by reducing the number of their employees or by cutting other expenses. These options are not available to you. Are you going to lay off yourself? Cutting some toy and supply expenses may save you a little money, but it won't be enough to offset the loss of clients.

So how can you compete? You can compete based on the quality of your program. To start, you must identify the benefits of your program and then share them with prospective clients.

Features versus Benefits

Your ability to answer the questions, "Why should I enroll my child in your program?" and "What does your program offer that other programs don't?" will largely determine how successful you will be at marketing your business. You may believe that you run a wonderful program, but unless parents also share this belief, you won't succeed; you must learn to immediately and consistently communicate the benefits of your program whenever parents ask those two questions.

Many providers do a poor job of communicating the benefits of their programs. When asked to describe her services, a provider might respond, "I'm a licensed provider. My program is open Monday through Friday from 6:00 a.m. to 6:00 p.m. I have a preschool opening, and I am on the Food Program." This answer gives parents few reasons to enroll their child. The provider has merely listed the features of her program, not the benefits. A feature describes what the provider offers. A benefit tells parents how their needs will be met by the provider. A feature focuses on the provider; a benefit focuses on the client.

Let's look again at the program description above and explore the differences between a feature and a benefit:

Feature	Benefit
"I am licensed."	"My program meets our state's highest health and safety standards to help ensure your child's safety."
"I'm open Monday through Friday from 6:00 a.m. to 6:00 p.m."	"I have convenient hours for a parent's work schedule."
"I'm on the Food Program."	"I serve nutritious meals that meet federal quality standards to help your child grow." (See page 130 for more information about the Food Program.)

Take time to understand the difference between a feature and a benefit. This is not an easy concept to master. As an exercise, look at what you've previously written about your program (in a classified ad, flyer, or parent handbook) and ask the question, "Why does this description matter to the parent or the child?" If your description doesn't clearly address the needs of your clients, then you've probably written a list of features, not benefits. Look again at the examples from the table above. Why does it matter to the client if the provider is licensed? A license indicates that a provider has met the state's health and safety standards. Parents don't care about licensing as much as they care about their child's health and safety, so the provider in the example should use these words when describing her program. Other key words in the table above are "convenient hours" and "nutritious meals." These are things that parents care about.

Your goal should be to identify three or four key benefits of your program. You should memorize them so you can repeat them at a moment's notice: when parents call, at a parent interview, or whenever someone asks about your program. Post these key benefits next to your telephone; list them in your business flyer and contract; include them in your newspaper advertising; publish them in your newsletter, on your website, and in your online classified ads; and include them in your enrollment packet. Your benefits are the answers to the two questions posed previously.

Getting Help Identifying Benefits

How can you identify the benefits of your program? Many providers struggle to come up with examples. Some providers are bashful about tooting their own horn. Here are some suggestions:

- When parents remove their child from your care, ask them to fill out a parent evaluation form (see appendix J for an example) so they can review what they liked about your program. They will probably use the language of benefits.

- Ask your current clients what they like best about the care you provide.

- Ask other providers or friends to give you feedback about your program.

- Ask your licensor (or regulator) what she feels is unique about your program. If the regulator has asked parents to evaluate providers, ask to see what the evaluations said.

- Survey parents who have used your program in past years. Ask what they remember most about your program.

- Ask the children in your care, "What do you like best about coming to my home?"

Once you have collected this information, you can tell a prospective client, "This is what other parents [or children] who have used my services like about my program." Then describe the benefits others have mentioned to you. Some providers find it easier to express themselves using this technique.

Try to come up with about ten initial benefits. Then weed out the benefits that most other providers could also claim (for example, serving nutritious meals and having convenient hours). If you have benefits that are special or unique, emphasize them. You may want to list ten benefits on a survey form and ask parents to choose the three that best describe your program. You also could ask for this information during the annual review of your contract and policies. In the end, choose three or four benefits to use on all of your marketing materials.

Examples of Benefits

At my training workshops, I often ask experienced providers, "What's the benefit of being in the child care business for many years?" Most providers answer, "Experience." No! You may have a lot of experience, but that doesn't mean you are a good teacher. We've all had experienced teachers who were also terrible teachers. Instead, I ask providers to come up with the benefit of their experience. The answer is *knowledge*. Tell parents how your experience has given you knowledge that will help their child learn:

- "I have seen many childhood illnesses, so I can help you quickly assess your child's health."

- "I know a lot about community resources, so I can refer you to services that can help you as a parent."

- "I have experience helping children with many different types of behavior issues, so I know I can respond appropriately to your child."

Here are some of the benefits new providers (who have been in business for less than a year) might communicate:

- "I have a lot of energy, and I am really excited about working with families."

- "I have lots of ideas about how to help children, and I listen closely to what parents want for their children."

- "My home is clean, and my toys are all new."

If you have a highly structured program, here's what you might say to promote your program's benefits:

- "Children need the structure of a schedule. The structure helps them feel comfortable and confident; they experience a stronger sense of control when they can predict what comes next."

On the other hand, if you have little structure in your program, you might promote your program this way:

- "I believe that young children learn through playing. I encourage children to explore many different activities at their own speed. I help children develop their curiosity and creativity, which are valuable skills that will help them throughout their lives."

When defining your benefits, emphasize the positive aspects of what you do. You don't need to criticize other programs and how they operate. If you do, you may become the target of negative criticism in return.

Our society is becoming more and more diverse in terms of race, religion, culture, ethnic background, and income level. It is important for all providers to understand this diversity when marketing their program. Learn more about your potential clients and take the time to ensure that your program is responsive to the needs of all current and potential clients. Be assertive in marketing diversity as a benefit of your program.

What Is High-Quality Care?

There are many ways to deliver high-quality child care. Here are some of the basic ingredients:

- The children are in a small group. They are properly supervised and given individualized care.

- The caregiver is reliable. The children develop a strong and stable relationship with the caregiver.

- The caregiver is responsive to the emotional and developmental needs of the children. The children can learn and grow at their own pace.

- There is effective communication between the caregiver and the parent. The children receive consistent messages.

- The environment is healthy and safe. The children are protected from hazardous conditions.

- The environment stimulates learning. It offers children enough space for exercise and exposes them to new ideas.

Notice how all of these ingredients focus on your program's impact on children and their success. The fundamental outcome of high-quality child care is that young children will learn skills and behaviors that will help them succeed in school and in life. Your benefits should help you communicate to parents that your primary concern is helping their children prepare for kindergarten. Parents want their children to learn, but they don't always associate learning with family child care.

Use the Language of Learning

To help parents understand how children will learn in your program, use the language of learning. Speak of yourself as a "teacher." You are, after all, the children's first teacher after their parents. Use words such as "learning," "teaching," and "tuition" with parents. Say things like, "I offer lots of opportunities for children to be creative so they can learn more." Always tell parents, "This is what your child learned today" and "This is what your child will learn tomorrow." You can't over-educate parents about what children are learning in your program. Here are some examples you can use with parents:

- Setting the table: Children are learning about counting. They are developing coordination skills by picking up and placing small objects. They are also learning about cooperating with others and being a part of a community.

- Dancing: Children are learning to understand simple movement directions. They are learning how to coordinate their entire body.

- Hearing stories at story time: Children are learning important literacy skills. They are learning to listen and retain information with their eyes and ears. They are recognizing words and pictures. They are also learning self-regulation by sitting and listening without interrupting.

For more examples, see appendix E, "Skills Children Learn in Family Child Care."

Learning is so important to parents because they want their children to succeed in school. Many child care programs (homes and centers) emphasize how they prepare children for school.

The Measure of Your Success

One of the best marketing ideas I have ever heard comes from a family child care provider in a small town in Wisconsin. Every spring the town newspaper prints the names of the upcoming graduates of the local high school and community college. This provider identifies which of these graduates once attended her child care program. She then runs an ad in the same newspaper with the headline, "Congratulations Graduates of the Busy Bee Family Child Care Program!" Under the headline, she lists the names of her former child care children who are graduating. What a powerful ad! She links achievement in education with her child care program; and all parents highly value education for their children. This child care provider sends a strong message by showing that children from her program have been successful in school—a positive outcome of learning in her family child care home. Is it reasonable for her to make this connection? Of course! This is a great way for her to tie her work with young children to their educational achievement later in life.

What is the measure of success for your program? It's how well the children do *after* leaving your program. Some parents will be afraid to enroll their child in your family child care program because they don't know what goes on in your home after they drop off their child. They don't know if their child is going to learn and grow. The prospective clients who come to your home for an interview probably will have diverse views on child discipline, teaching techniques, religion, and child-rearing philosophies. You are alone at home with their child, so, based on their background, they might be nervous about whether you're the best caregiver for their unique child. As a family child care provider, you want to tell prospective clients that their child will do well in your program. You can reassure these parents that they need not fear about individual differences in your program. One of the best ways to do this is to show them how well children in your program—from diverse backgrounds—succeed in school and life after they leave your program. That's the measure of your success.

Keep track of children after they leave your program. Write letters and send birthday cards. Ask the children to write letters back and to send you pictures of themselves. Collect pictures of them graduating from high school or college. Collect pictures of their weddings, new jobs, growing families, and any other major life changes. Do this for as long as you are in business.

Post the pictures and letters on the wall or in your scrapbook or photo album. (Be sure to get their permission!) When prospective parents visit your home, tell them that you've cared for many other children of parents like them and that these children are turning out fine. You might say, "Here's Billy, who is in high school now and on the swimming team. I got a letter from him last month, and here's the picture he sent of himself at a swim meet." You might say, "Here's Lucinda, who recently got married and is working in a local bank" or "Here's Maria, who got straight As in her first year at Saint Louis University." After showing the parents some of these photos, end by saying, "I'm sure your child would also do well if enrolled in my program."

Pictures and letters from former clients and their children are powerful statements of how well you did your job. When parents see the ongoing connection you have with the families in your care, they will understand that these are the important things in life, not the small differences between you that might exist today. Parents—along with their children—will want to be a part of such a lifelong relationship. (Of course, if a child who was once in your program ends up in jail, you would take down any pictures of that child!)

Another way to show how well the children from your program do in life is to get testimonials from their kindergarten teachers after they leave your program. Talk to these kindergarten teachers and ask them how prepared your child care children were as compared to other children. Urge them to write you a letter describing how well the children from your program are doing. Such letters can be used as a powerful tool to help parents overcome any doubts about whether their child will be ready for school after your program.

Are You a Preschool Program?

Many parents look for a "preschool" program for their young children. To them, preschool is a structured learning program that follows a set curriculum and is offered during part of the day. Parents like preschools because they associate them with learning. Many family child care providers don't offer a preschool program, but they do care for preschool-age children. If that's the case for you, always communicate to parents how their preschooler will learn in your program. Tell parents things like this:

- "I offer a program for preschoolers with planned, age-appropriate learning activities geared to each child's interests."

- "My curriculum is designed to meet the individual needs of each child."

- "I offer a home environment where children feel safe and comfortable— a place that will prepare your child to succeed when he enters the school system."

The language parents hear from you is important. You don't want a parent to turn away from your services just because you don't say the word "preschool" when describing your program. Having said this, if you don't offer the structured environment of a preschool, don't pretend that you do. Instead, simply communicate to parents how children learn in your program. Don't apologize to parents if you don't offer a preschool program. Children can learn in both less structured and more structured learning environments.

Use Clear Language When Stating Benefits

When developing your list of benefits, don't use complicated words or jargon. Benefits should be stated using clean, understandable language. Instead of saying, "I use developmentally appropriate toys," say, "I give children toys that are challenging and fun for their age." Here are some other examples of clearly communicated benefits:

- "My program is available for children of all ages, including infants, so parents don't have to separate siblings."
- "I care for mildly ill children so parents won't have to miss work."
- "I have a Child Development Associate (CDA) credential or an advanced degree in early childhood education; I apply my increased knowledge to help your child learn."
- "I am an experienced preschool teacher who offers a child-centered curriculum with planned learning activities and weekly themes."
- "I interact closely with parents and am supportive of families."
- "My program is close to a state park, public swimming pool, or playground where your child will have fun."
- "My program is close to your home, so you will spend less time traveling."
- "Age-appropriate computer programs are available for children ages three years and older, with screen time limited."
- "My family child care home has an enclosed yard for safe, fun outdoor activities."
- "I am an energetic mother who loves children."
- "I provide an enrichment program in a foreign language or another culture."

- "I instruct children in etiquette; children learn good manners."
- "My program has flexible hours to meet parents' busy schedules."
- "I am a former dance instructor, nurse, singer, actor, or musician."
- "I am a grandmother who has raised eleven of her own children."
- "My program serves home-cooked, nutritious meals."
- "My program is in a home environment where children feel safe and comfortable."
- "My home-based program offers individual care and attention."
- "My program offers informal, noninstitutional family care."
- "I teach religious or nonreligious moral ethics that introduce children to moral values."
- "I am a male caregiver, which helps children from female-headed families learn to bond with male adults."
- "My program meets the highest national quality standards by being accredited by the National Association for Family Child Care (NAFCC)."
- "My program allows only limited television viewing."
- "My program includes children from mixed-age groups (and sibling care) so children can help teach each other and learn from those older than they are."
- "My multicultural program educates children about different cultures."
- "My program is open twenty-four hours a day and provides flexible hours to meet the needs of parents."
- "I give piano lessons to teach music appreciation."
- "My program's planned activities are geared to each child's interests."
- "I plan events with other providers to increase opportunities for children to socialize with their peers."
- "I regularly organize field trips in the community (such as nature walks and visits to local businesses) so children are exposed to new places and things."
- "The small group size of my program means your child will receive more individual attention, which will help your child learn."
- "My program specializes in infant, toddler, or school-age care."

- "I am a stable, dependable provider, so you won't have to worry about needing a backup caregiver."
- "I rotate a variety of stimulating toys and learning activities throughout the year so children won't get bored."

You can find online a list of hundreds of benefits from family child care providers who have posted them on their Provider's Choice of Minnesota web pages: www .providerschoice.com/pages/mnchildcare.

Affordable Rates

There is a perception among many parents that family child care is less expensive than child care centers. Many providers do charge less than centers, but some charge more. Although it might make sense for some providers in highly competitive areas to market themselves as less expensive than their competition, in general, it is not a good idea for providers to compete on this basis. If more providers start competing with lower prices, all providers' rates will be driven down. The average rates charged in a community will be lower, which will reduce the number of providers who will receive government subsidies for low-income parents. Instead, let's create a new impression among parents that a family child care program is a place to find high-quality care, not a place to find lower rates. See chapter 9 for more information about setting your rates.

You Can Compete with Any Program

No program can offer everything for every child's needs. Don't be discouraged if you see other programs that offer benefits you don't have. You also offer benefits that others do not. You might be closer to a park, have more experience with infants, or offer longer hours. Your program can also compete with any child care center. Below is a list of benefits from a major chain of child care centers, taken directly from its national website. Read these benefits and think about how your program compares:

- age-appropriate curriculum created by a university early childhood education program
- high standards of security and safety

- flexible hours: 6:30 a.m. to 6:00 p.m.
- college-trained teachers
- hot meals and two snacks served daily
- safe, insured transportation
- parent open-door policy
- state-of-the-art facilities

You probably offer many of these same benefits, such as high standards of safety, flexible hours, hot meals and two snacks, safe transportation, and an open-door policy. You may have some training credentials that compare well to those of a child care center teacher, and your home might have a security system. What's the benefit of a state-of-the-art facility? It's not clear. If you have well-designed play areas for children with child-sized furniture and plenty of toys and other stimulating activities, then your home is also state of the art. Many early childhood care and education experts say that a home environment is usually better for children than a commercial institution.

What about the curriculum designed by an early childhood education department? Can you compete here? Absolutely. Perhaps you use a curriculum program, such as the *Family Child Care Curriculum* (Redleaf Press) or *The Creative Curriculum for Family Child Care* (Teaching Strategies). Many other curriculum guides are suitable for use in family child care as well. Instead, maybe you use a child-centered format that is an excellent way to organize learning experiences for young children. You might just also rely on your experiential knowledge gained from applying child-development theory into your daily practice for many years. Your program may have a variety of other benefits the list above does not include. For example, you may offer an enrichment program in a foreign language. For more information about how to compete with centers, see pages 163–65.

Identifying and communicating the benefits of your program to parents should be the cornerstone of your marketing efforts. Be confident; your benefits will attract parents to your program.

CHAPTER 3

Marketing to Prospective Clients

Your most important prospective clients—to whom you should promote your program—are parents who are looking for child care. This chapter will discuss how to market to prospective clients. To begin, let's take a look at how to make a good first impression and then consider some additional marketing strategies to attract parents to your program.

You want to make a good first impression when parents contact you. The three most important contact times with prospective clients are

1 when they first see your home;

2 when they first call you on the phone; and

3 when they come to your home for an interview.

On the three occasions listed above, don't give parents a reason not to enroll their child with you—a reason such as your car in the driveway has a flat tire, you sound distracted over the phone, or your television is tuned to a reality show when they visit your home. In your first contacts with parents, try to identify their needs, communicate your program's benefits quickly and clearly, and make the parents feel comfortable. As a marketer, your job is to convince prospective parents that you are providing a solution to their problem. This requires skill in handling people as well as skill in using written materials to explain your program. This chapter describes how you can develop both.

Be sure to keep track of how parents learned about your program. Measure the effectiveness of your promotional activities—such as distributing keepsakes and business flyers, participating in local parades, or spreading positive word of mouth—by using the Parent Call Tracking Form in appendix C.

The Appearance of Your Home

First impressions matter in every business, but especially in yours. Make sure that what parents see, outside and inside your home, makes a positive impression. Prepare your home as if you were selling it (which, in a way, you are). Walk around the front of your home and into the entryway. Do you think parents will want to leave their child here? Keep in mind this checklist for presenting your home as a clean, safe, and inviting environment:

- [ ] Make sure your home's street number is clearly visible from the road so parents can find you easily.
- [ ] Mow your lawn and pull weeds regularly.
- [ ] Keep your house freshly painted, your screens in good repair, and your brickwork mortared.
- [ ] Keep your dog behind a secure fence.
- [ ] Plant flowers in the front yard or display flower boxes in the windows or on the porch.
- [ ] Clean the front windows often.
- [ ] Put away yard tools and garden hoses.
- [ ] Store leaves in decorative lawn bags.
- [ ] Take in newspapers and mail right away.
- [ ] If your car is parked out front, keep it clean inside and out.
- [ ] Look at the back of your house and your alley (if you have one). Clean things up, including any overflowing garbage cans.
- [ ] If you have a business sign in your front yard, make sure it is in good shape.
- [ ] Examine the entryway of your home. Parents should feel welcome, comfortable, and safe when they first walk into your home. Here are some touches that will create a welcome feeling:

— Have some items (children's drawings or photographs) posted at a child's level to make children feel welcome.

— Make the entryway the cleanest area of your home. Put away all clutter. Although your play areas are likely to be filled with toys, keep the entryway clean.

☐ Eliminate bad odors from cooking, dirty diapers, or pets by using an unscented odor neutralizer (some people are allergic to fragrance sprays).

☐ Post photos of children, your credentials, and a schedule of activities on a nearby bulletin board. Take down notices reminding parents to pay you.

☐ Turn off the television and don't have any music playing.

☐ Keep pets away from children.

☐ Have your enrollment packet readily available.

Once you've completed the actions above, ask a friend with young children to come over and tour the outside and entryway of your home and give you feedback. An objective point of view can give you a fresh perspective.

You may want to read *Family Child Care Homes: Creative Spaces for Children to Learn* by Linda Armstrong (published by Redleaf Press). It contains a lot of ideas and examples of how to make your home look inviting to children and their families. It includes full-color photos and illustrations and is a wonderful resource for both new and experienced providers.

Telephone Contact

Most prospective clients will contact you by phone. Just as with the appearance of your home, that first phone call is an opportunity to give families a favorable impression of your program.

Recorded Telephone Greeting

When a parent calls you at your place of business and you can't answer the phone, you don't want to lose the call. If your phone rings and rings and you don't have an answering machine or voice mail service to record a message, prospective clients will call another provider (and current clients will worry!). Therefore, it is imperative that you have an answering machine or voice mail service with a recorded greeting from you asking parents to leave a message. Your recorded greeting should leave a positive, professional impression on the caller. A greeting that has children crying in the background or a garbled message will alienate the caller. Instead, leave a greeting that explains you can't answer the phone because you are with the children. This statement of your priority will impress most parents. Here are some additional suggestions:

- In the greeting, identify the name of your business. You might say, for example, "Hello! You have reached April's Playhouse and the Beckman residence. This is April Beckman. No one can come to the phone right now because we are busy with the children. Please leave a message with your name and phone number, and we will call you back as soon as we can. Thank you very much for calling." You could also add, "For further information about my program, please visit my website at . . . ."

- If you want to keep your business and personal messages separate, purchase a telephone answering machine or service that allows you to record messages in two different places. Your greeting might now say, "Hello! You have reached April's Playhouse and the Beckman residence. This is April Beckman. If you would like to leave a message for April's Playhouse, press 1 now. If you would like to leave a message for April, Bill, Sylvia, or Brian, press 2 now." A parent who presses 1 would then hear the rest of your business greeting.

- Announce the age groups that you have openings for in your greeting. You might say, "Currently I have an opening for one toddler and will have a preschool opening on September 1." If the parent is looking for an infant opening, she will not need to leave a message. This will save time for both her and you.

- Purchase a second phone line to use for all business calls. Although the cost of the first phone line into your home is not tax deductible, the business portion of a second line is. It doesn't matter if your phones are cellular or connected to a landline.

- As long as they speak clearly and the message is short, you could have your own child or the children in your care deliver the greeting. Be sure to get permission from parents before you use their child's voice. (See appendix K, "Photo, Voice, Website, Facebook, and Video Permission Form.")

- Don't use a commercial greeting service featuring impersonations of famous people. Don't use an exotic or silly greeting. These are neither professional nor reassuring, and they may offend some people.

- Make sure parents can leave a long message. Don't use an answering machine or voice mail service that cuts off after only one minute.

- Make sure your greeting starts playing after no more than three unanswered rings. Don't make parents wait and wait before they can leave a message.

- To reduce the number of unanswered calls, get a cell phone to carry with you to the backyard and on field trips. Some providers also have car phones and pagers. You can forward calls from your house line to your cell phone when you are out of the house. (Note: The business portion of such telephone equipment is tax deductible.)

- After recording your greeting, ask a friend to call your number, listen to the message, and give you constructive feedback. You want to sound clear, positive, and energetic. If you smile while recording your greeting, you will communicate friendliness.

- Tell parents that if they call you during the day, they will probably get your answering machine. Reassure them that you check often for messages and that you will return their calls promptly. Establish times when you will be easy to reach so parents know the best times to call.

- Because you are in the business of caring for children, try to keep all phone calls short during business hours so you don't take your attention away from the children.

In some parts of the country, telephone companies may treat providers as commercial customers and charge them a higher commercial rate on their monthly phone bill. Despite this, it is still worthwhile to record a business greeting.

How to Handle Phone Calls from Prospective Clients

Every phone call from a prospective client has the potential to create new business. And it offers you the chance to make a good first impression. How you handle each call is very important. Some parents sound very organized over the phone, and their questions are specific. Other parents may not be sure what to ask you. The questions every parent wants answered are, "Will this program meet the needs of my child and my family?" and "Is there something special about this program that might sway me toward enrolling my child?" Because of this, you need to be an active, not passive, communicator on the phone. Rather than just responding to what a parent asks you, you should take charge of the phone conversation by asking questions. You should be the one who decides whether or not you want the parent to come over for an interview. Assume the attitude that you are choosing the parent, not that you are waiting for the parent to choose you. Follow this three-step process for every parent phone call:

1   Find out the specific needs of the parent and the child.

2   Briefly describe the benefits of your program.

3   Get the parent to agree to come over to your house for an interview.

In step one, determining the specific needs of the parent and the child, your goal is to quickly assess whether your program can meet those needs. If it cannot, don't spend any more time on the phone than necessary before you politely tell the parent that your program isn't a good fit for the child's needs. To determine a family's needs, start by asking questions about the child:

- "How old is your child?"
- "What are your child's needs?"
- "What hours do you need care?"
- "What does your child enjoy doing?"
- "What are you looking for in a program for your child?"

By asking such questions, you can help the parent relax while you listen for any major issues indicating that your program is not a good fit. If you think things won't work out, don't hesitate to decide against enrolling the child. In this case, tell the parent, "I don't think my program can meet the needs of your child as you have described them. I think you should look for another caregiver. Thank you for calling." You might want to refer this parent to another provider or to your local child care resource and referral (CCR&R) agency. See page 43 for more information on how to say no to a parent.

If the parent sounds promising, move on to step two: briefly describing the key benefits of your program. You might say, "I offer a structured program that prepares children to enter their school years eager to learn. I have a large backyard where children can run and play and have a lot of fun." Then share with the parent the top three benefits of your program. Try to relate your program's benefits to the needs previously expressed by the parent. In other words, if the parent has said his child enjoys learning about nature, you might describe your regular field trips to a nearby park. Don't be afraid to express how proud you are of what you do.

There is no single way to handle a phone interview. Some providers prefer to say as little as possible about their program over the phone. Once these providers have decided they can meet the parent's needs, their only goal is to get the parent to come over for an interview. Many providers believe that the best way to market their business is in person, face-to-face. They believe that the more they describe their services over the phone, the more likely they are to turn off a prospective client. For example, a parent might think the provider is too far away, but after coming over and seeing the program, she decides she is willing to make the trip. A parent might want to spend $180 a week tops, but after meeting the provider, she decides she is willing to pay $195. A provider might have a terrific curriculum, but this can't be demonstrated over the phone. When a parent calls, she might be looking for an answer to one particular question; if the provider gives the wrong answer, the parent might not want to come over for an interview. To avoid this problem, some providers simply don't discuss the details of their program on the phone. Instead, they convey to the parent that he has to see her program before he can make a decision.

Step three is to get the parent to agree to come to your home for an interview. This is the ultimate goal of every phone call from a prospective client. Invite parents to your home by asking a question they can't say no to. For example, say, "Would you like to visit next Tuesday or Wednesday?" rather than asking, "Would you like to make an appointment for an interview?" If the parent can't decide whether to schedule an interview, tell him that you'll call back in a day or two after he has had time to think about it. It is important to schedule the interview as soon as possible (within three or four days), because parents may have already scheduled interviews with other providers. Here are some tips for handling parent phone calls:

- Place the phone where loud noises from child care children and other distractions are minimal.

- Explain to the children in your care that you need to have quiet time when you are on the phone.

- Place the following items by each phone in your home so you are ready to handle phone calls:

  — a pen or pencil

  — the Parent Call Tracking Form (see appendix C)

  — a list of your top three program benefits

- Answer all phone calls with a business, not personal, greeting. For example, you might say, "Hello, Juanita's Little Steps Child Care. This is Juanita. May I help you?" Don't answer the phone by saying, "Hello?" or "Yeah?" or "Juanita's residence."

- At the very start of your conversation, ask for the parent's name, mailing address, phone number, and e-mail address. Next, ask for the names and ages of the children for whom she is seeking care and how she heard about your program. Use this opportunity to track the effectiveness of your promotions and advertising. If the parent mentions the name of someone who referred her to you, record this name and send a thank-you note later. Remembering to ask for this information is easy if you use the "Parent Call Tracking Form" in appendix C.

- When talking with the parent, always try to sound positive and maintain an upbeat tone of voice. Smile while you are speaking. You will sound friendlier. How you sound on the phone is as important as what you say.

- Don't interact with child care children while you are on the phone. If a situation demands your attention, excuse yourself, deal quickly with the issue, and then finish the call.

- If you are very busy or having a bad day, you may not want to answer the phone. In this situation, let your answering machine or voice mail record parent calls. Return calls when it is more convenient and you are more in control. If you do answer the phone when you are distracted, ask for the parent's name and phone number and tell him you will call back when it's more convenient for you. For example, say, "Thank you for calling. I'm in the middle of an activity with the children right now. May I call you back in a few minutes? I appreciate your understanding. At what number can I reach you?" Parents are more likely to be impressed that the children are your first priority than upset that you can't talk right away. It's best to talk with parents only when you can give them your full attention and when you are feeling confident about yourself and your program. If you can't call back right away, give the parent a realistic time when you can return the call. Then fulfill your promise.

- If other members of your family answer the phone, discuss with them how you want them to handle business calls. Ask them to be courteous, friendly, and helpful. They might say, "Hello, this is the Wang residence and Yei's Child Care. This is Justin speaking. May I help you? . . . No, my mother can't come to the phone right now because she is with the children. May I take your name and number and have her call you back shortly?"

- After the phone call is over, send a thank-you note or postcard to the parent, even if it is obvious that he will not enroll his child in your program. If you have scheduled the parent for an interview, send a thank-you note along with a "Choosing Child Care Checklist" (see appendix F). Send your business flyer and a reminder notice a few days before the interview.

Should You Discuss Rates over the Phone?

"How much do you charge?" is a difficult question to answer on the phone. Some providers will answer this question clearly and directly; others will tell parents they must come for an interview before discussing rates. There is no simple answer that works for everyone. Of course, you don't want to lose a potential client based on your rates before you've had a chance to promote your program. On the other hand, you don't want to spend several hours in an interview only to have the parent decline enrollment because your rates are over her budget. Some providers explain that they can't discuss their rates easily over the phone because they offer incentives or discounts depending on circumstances (such as for military families, families enrolling multiple children, and so on); they explain that discussing these issues is less difficult in person.

Some providers respond to this question by saying, "I'm not the most expensive or the least expensive child care program." Some providers tell parents they will mail them a copy of their rate schedule. Some direct parents to their website, where rates and other fees are posted. Other providers are very straightforward about discussing their rates on the phone; they want to weed out those parents who are simply price shopping. Any of these options are authoritative and professional ways to communicate.

One provider I know tells callers, "I'm not the cheap alternative. If you are looking for the cheapest care, you should keep looking. I have a master's degree in early childhood education and seven years of experience in caring for young children, and I use a planned curriculum that promotes the learning and emotional development of the children. I would be happy to schedule an interview with you and your child. I have time next Monday or Tuesday evening. Which would work best for you?"

Another provider, who doesn't give her rates over the phone, told me about a parent who came to her several weeks after enrolling his child. He said, "When I first started looking for child care, I had a set amount I was willing to pay. After our interview in your home, I saw how much you had to offer my child, and I decided I was willing to pay more for quality. If you had told me your rates over the phone, I probably wouldn't have followed up." Sometimes parents ask questions about rates because they don't know what other questions to ask! This is another reason to take charge of the conversation by asking questions of the parent and communicating the benefits of your program. For a further discussion of rates, see chapter 9.

No matter what you say, don't be defensive when discussing rates. If a parent complains about your rates, don't try too hard to justify them. You could explain that the value of your service comes from the benefits you offer: "My rates are based on the knowledge I've gained from my five years of experience as a provider, my

CDA credential, and the variety of special field trips we take each month." There will always be parents who can't afford your services, so don't push too hard when explaining why you charge what you charge. It's best to keep your message simple when you share your rates.

Occasionally you may get a call from a parent who is in a hurry to enroll her child after talking with you for only a few minutes. How do you handle this situation? First, you should be hesitant to enroll any child without a face-to-face interview. Invite the parent and the child for an interview as soon as possible. If the parent refuses to come to an interview and insists that you agree to enroll her child right away, this is a bad sign and you should probably not consent. If the parent needs care immediately, you may want to enroll the child on a drop-in basis and charge by the day for the first two weeks to see how it works out. Make it clear that your daily rate will cost more per week than your normal weekly rate (see chapter 9).

If you are getting parent calls but few parents are accepting your invitation for an interview, it's time to evaluate what you are doing. Think about what you might be saying—or how you might be saying it—that could be causing parents to turn you down. Go over several recent phone conversations with a friend and ask for suggestions on what you could do differently. If you don't have trouble getting parents to come over for interviews but you find most of them unacceptable for enrollment, try to think of ways you could better screen parents on the phone so you don't waste so much time with interviews.

Talking about Special Needs

Under the Americans with Disabilities Act (ADA), discriminating against a parent or a child who has a disability is illegal. What do you do if the parent tells you on the phone that his child has a disability, such as asthma, epilepsy, attention deficit disorder, or AIDS? Here are some tips:

- You are required to do what a reasonable person would do to provide appropriate care for the child. You are not required to provide care if doing so would be significantly difficult or significantly expensive. You are not required to provide care if doing so would fundamentally alter the nature of your program. Therefore, you cannot say, "I don't provide care for children with disabilities" or "I don't provide care for children who use a wheelchair." You must consider the needs of each child and explore how you could offer appropriate care. You cannot charge more to care for children with special needs. Do not decline to conduct an interview with a parent simply because the child has a disability. If you do so, you could be in violation of the ADA.

- Ask the parent on the phone and at the interview what kind of accommodations, if any, the child may need to be a part of your program. If you are not sure how you can provide appropriate care for the child, ask questions. Seek help from outside resources, such as a public health nurse, your regulatory worker, or your CCR&R agency.

- You should look upon caring for children with special needs as a business opportunity. Parents are trying to find someone to care for their child; they are not looking to sue you. Many providers have been caring for children who have a variety of disabilities for many years without problems. There are a growing number of children with special needs who need child care. The more experience you have with caring for such children, the more you can successfully market yourself to this audience. You may want to promote yourself by saying, "We welcome special needs children" or "I have five years of experience caring for children with a variety of special needs. I've been very successful at incorporating children with special needs into my program, and all the children have benefited from this experience." For more information about the ADA, see the *Family Child Care Legal and Insurance Guide* (published by Redleaf Press).

How to Handle Interviews with Parents

The parent interview is probably your most important opportunity to market your business. Make sure you are doing everything you can to make a good impression. Here are three goals you should pursue at every parent interview:

1 Determine whether the parent's and the child's needs are a good match for your program.

2   Explain the benefits of your program.

3   Ask the parent to enroll in your program.

Should you conduct a parent interview in the evening or during your business hours? Should the child be present at the interview? Should both parents (if there are two) be present? Not all providers answer these questions the same way. Evening interviews are often more convenient for parents (and you!) and allow time for discussion without distractions. Evening interviews, however, do not give parents an opportunity see your program in action. If the child is present for the interview, you can better evaluate if he will be a good match with the other children. At the same time, the child could be distracting and make your discussion with the parents more difficult. In a two-parent family, having both parents attend the parent interview is crucial. If one parent doesn't have time to participate in this important discussion, it may indicate that the parent won't have time to help you deal with other issues later on.

Providers handle parent interviews in a variety of ways; there is no one way that works best for everyone. Some conduct only one interview with parents. Others conduct their parent interviews in two stages: First, the provider meets in the evening with just the parents, answers questions, and gives a tour of the home. If both parties are still interested, a second meeting is scheduled with the parents and the child during business hours to see if the child will fit in. Some providers even visit the parental home for a final interview to learn about the child's home environment and to see how the child interacts with her parents. Here are some tips to consider for your parent interview:

- Call the parent a few days before the interview to confirm the appointment. If you have already sent a postcard reminder, you may not want to call. If you do call, say that you look forward to his visit. If the parent wants to cancel the interview, thank him for his interest. Ask him to reconsider your program at a future time.

- In preparation for the interview, make sure your house looks orderly. Make the beds and do the dishes. Your home should look like a place that is friendly to children, so don't overclean by putting away all the toys.

- Dress comfortably.

- Set up a space in a quiet area of your home to sit down and have an extended conversation with parents. Ask your family members not to disturb you during the interview. If the interview is conducted during your business hours, have a helper or family member take charge of the children at this time.

- Spend a little time talking and playing with the new child, but don't come on too strong. Tell the parent, "If I seem to be ignoring your child, it's because I like to let children come to me instead of pouncing on them." At the end of the interview, you might want to give the child a small present (possibly a keepsake, see page 86) and a certificate to celebrate her visit to your program.

- Have an open mind at the start of each interview. At the beginning of the interview, make it clear to the parents that both they and you have to agree to enroll their child. Sometimes parents think that it's just up to them. Don't hesitate to turn a parent down if you believe conflicts with the parent or child might be too hard for you to handle.

- Rather than describing your program in detail right away, you may want to start by asking the parents if they have any initial questions. Listen carefully to the parents' needs and concerns. Take notes if this will help you remember them more easily. Respond to any specific issues raised by a parent. Parents who have their questions answered first are more likely to feel at ease and be receptive to you and your program.

- Review appendix D, the "Parent Interview Checklist." Keep a copy of the completed checklist for your files. (If you put the parent on your waiting list, refer to this checklist again before enrolling the child.)

- Ask open-ended questions to help you identify parent and child needs. An open-ended question is one that cannot be answered with a simple yes or no. For example, you might say, "What would be the most important thing I could do to help your child grow?" or "What are your child's special interests?" or "What do you see your child doing in three months, one year, or five years?" This last question can help you identify parents' expectations for their child. Point out how your program can meet those expectations.

- Present the parents with a package of written materials about your program. Arrange these materials in a colorful folder, possibly with your business name on the front. Have one package available for each parent. Your package might include the following:
    — a business card for each parent
    — a business flyer
    — the "Choosing Child Care Checklist" (see appendix F)
    — a description of your child caring philosophy
    — references from current or previous clients
    — your background credentials, such as your years of experience, training credentials, and educational degrees
    — your contract and policies, which should describe your rates, payment policies, hours, daily schedule, paid vacations, and holidays
    — an enrollment form for parents to sign
    — sample menus from the Food Program

Tour of Your Home

Give the parent a tour of your home/business. As you walk through the playroom, bedrooms, kitchen, and other areas, emphasize that your home is a safe place for children. Parents think about their children's safety above all else, so this is the most important thing you can highlight. Point out all the safety features of your home; what is obvious to you may not be obvious for all parents. Here are some examples of what you might point out and say:

- "All electrical outlets are covered to protect the children."
- "I always make sure that dangerous household chemicals and objects are locked behind these cupboards or doors to keep the children safe."
- "We have child-sized furniture and pillows so the children can feel comfortable and safe."
- "To prevent injuries if children fall, the floors in this room are carpeted and there are no sharp edges on the furniture."
- "Notice the gates at the front of the stairs to keep toddlers at bay."
- "Here are our smoke detectors and fire extinguishers."

- "I conduct a monthly fire and tornado drill with the children, in compliance with licensing laws."

Your home tour shouldn't focus entirely on safety issues, of course. Your home tour should also emphasize that you have a fun and creative place for children to learn in. Here are some other things to point out that show the benefits of your program:

- "We have a variety of toys and books available for the children. We rotate toys from storage every few months so the children don't get bored."
- "We keep the curtains open to create a well-lit, cheerful atmosphere that the children enjoy."
- "We serve nutritious meals, including breakfast, a morning snack, lunch, and an afternoon snack."
- "I sit in this chair rocking babies every day."
- "Here is where I read to the children in the afternoon every day."
- "Our outdoor equipment is constantly used by the children. It helps them to exercise and have fun."

If you have prepared a scrapbook or photo album that illustrates various aspects of your program, show it to the parents and their children.

After you have finished the tour of your home and you've answered all the parents' questions, it is time to make a decision. If you want to enroll the child, ask the parents, "Are you ready to make a decision to enroll your child at this time, or do you need a few days to think about it? If you can decide today, I have the paperwork here for you to fill out." If the parent is not ready to make a decision, ask, "Is there anything else I can do to help you make a decision today?" If the parent needs more time, say, "When do you think you will be able to make a decision? Can I call you at that time?" Give the parents a specific deadline by which to make a decision. If you have other prospective parents who are interested in your program, you should tell the parent this. If the parent does not call you by the deadline, call her to confirm that she is not interested. Setting a deadline allows you to quickly fill your openings rather than be kept waiting by a parent.

Sometimes you will decide that you do not want to enroll a child, and you have every right not to. Remind the parents that both you and they have to agree that the program is a good fit before the child can be enrolled. Be sensitive when you say no to parents; you want them to leave without feeling negative about your program, for you don't want them speaking ill of your program to other potential clients. On page 43, you will find a more detailed discussion about how to say no to enrolling a child.

If you are conducting a lot of interviews but enrolling few parents, evaluate how you handle your interviews. Was your home presentable? Did the parents show signs of disapproval about things you said? Did they object to anything in your contract or any of your policies? Maybe your hours were not flexible enough or parents were concerned you did not have a "preschool" program (see page 18). After a number of unsuccessful interviews, you may want to seek help and advice from an experienced provider.

If you are nervous about conducting interviews with parents, role-play the entire process with a friend. Ask the friend for honest feedback: Were you friendly? Did you put her at ease? Did you ask specific questions about her needs? Did you clearly explain your program's benefits? Did you ask directly for her to enroll her child? Sometimes all it takes to conduct a good interview is practice.

Follow-Up Contacts

Sometimes a prospective client will call or visit your program and then fail to contact you again. There are many reasons why a parent may drop out of contact. The parent may have called a number of providers and can't make up her mind; the parent may have decided not to change her current child care arrangement for now; or the parent may have chosen another provider. With an increasing number of child care options to choose from, some parents have trouble differentiating one provider from another and get stuck in trying to make a child care decision. Because of this, following up every time a parent contacts you is critical. Here are some tips:

- Always ask prospective parents for their phone number, address, and e-mail address when they first call.

- After they call or come for an interview, send them a short thank-you note by e-mail. Tell them you appreciate their spending time with you.

- If you send a follow-up letter, write it by hand. Your service is too personal to send a form letter. You may want to enclose a keepsake with your note (see page 86).

- Ask parents for permission to give them a follow-up call within a week.

If after sending a note, you don't hear back from a parent, always make a follow-up call! It should be your policy to always follow up with parents. Start your conversation by saying, "We spoke a while ago about your search for child care. I'm calling to find out whether you have found care for your daughter, Elana." If the parent responds that she has not found a suitable child care arrangement, reply, "Is there anything I can do to help you further?" Offer another brief reminder about one of your program's benefits, such as, "We are going on a field trip to the zoo next month, which I am sure Elana would enjoy." Because so few providers make follow-up calls, a simple offer of help may convince a parent to enroll in your program.

If the parent responds that she has found another child care arrangement, ask what made her choose that program. Take notes about the reasons. This information may help you with the next prospective parent who contacts you. By asking this question, you will learn about what is important to parents who are looking for child care. Parents will usually use the language of benefits when they answer. If the parent says she chose another program because it was closer to her home or because the other person is a relative, there is nothing you can do. But if the parent mentions that the other program has more toys or less clutter or has a backyard fence, then you might consider these suggestions for how you could change your program.

At the end of such a conversation—no matter how the parent responds to your question—thank the parent for his time. Close the conversation by saying, "If you run into other parents who are looking for child care in the area, I would appreciate your giving them my contact information." Parents with young children often know other parents with young children. Don't be afraid to ask for such a referral! It's reasonable to ask this parent for a referral because he already knows something about your program. Tell the parent you will e-mail him a brief flyer about your program that he can forward to any prospective clients he knows. You may even want to offer this parent a finder's fee for a successful referral (see page 58). If you prepare newsletters for your current clients, send a copy of your latest newsletter, your business card, and a brief thank-you note to this prospective parent as well. If the parent has found another caregiver, mention that you are available to do backup care or sick care if his current child care provider goes on vacation or becomes ill.

Conducting follow-up calls costs you nothing, and it's a good way to encourage positive word-of-mouth marketing for your program. It will make you stand out.

Other Marketing Strategies

The appearance of your home, communicating effectively over the phone, conducting successful interviews, and following up are all important marketing strategies, but there are many other ways to market yourself and your business to prospective clients.

Be a Good Neighbor

Before you start your child care business, check your local zoning ordinances, homeowners association bylaws, restrictive covenants, or rental agreements to make sure you are not prohibited from operating a child care business. (See my book *Family Child Care Legal and Insurance Guide* for information on how to respond to restrictive ordinances and covenants.) Assuming you are entitled to run a business from your home, announce to the neighbors on your block that you are about to begin caring for children in your home. You can do this by dropping off your business flyer or by placing a door hanger on their front doorknob. A better way might be to stop by and talk with each neighbor individually. Listen to any neighborhood concerns and head off complaints before they become serious. Neighbors who are rude to your families or who complain to child care regulators can create problems.

Neighbors may be unhappy about having a child care program nearby for several reasons; they might be worried about noise, parking issues, safety, their property value, and the appearance of your yard, among other things. If you are open to talking about these issues with your neighbors, they shouldn't be permanent obstacles. First, tell your neighbors about your plans for your business. Be especially clear about the maximum number of children you will care for and the hours you will be open. Some neighbors may imagine that you will have thirty children in your home. Reassure them that there will always be fewer children than this in your home at any one time. Because of the small numbers involved, noise is usually not a problem. Remind neighbors that you will be home every day and can keep a protective eye on the neighborhood. If you plan to offer second-shift or overnight care, prepare a brief list of rules for your families to follow (for example, no car-door slamming or horn honking to announce their arrival), and share this list with your neighbors. Ask them what else you could do to help keep noise down.

Parking concerns are usually not a problem in family child care. Inform neighbors that only a few cars will stop by twice a day. If you care for more than one child in a family, point out that even fewer cars will drive by. If you have limited space for parking, ask parents to stagger their drop-off and pickup times if possible. Inform parents never to block or use a neighbor's driveway. Safety concerns can be addressed by telling neighbors that you have liability insurance, that you will strictly follow all child care regulations, and that you will use common sense. Ask your neighbors if they have any specific safety questions so you can respond with a plan to address them.

There is little evidence that property values are affected by family child care programs. Ask your local property tax office or real estate agent for information on this. If you are concerned that local laws may restrict the operation of your family child care business, have a friend call the local property tax office under the pretext of doing research, and have the information mailed to your friend's address. At the very least, reassure neighbors that you also have an interest in keeping property values up and mention that some families will likely want to live in a neighborhood with a child care provider nearby. Acknowledge that nobody—including you—wants to live next to someone with a messy, unkempt yard. Keep your play area tidy every day. You may want to put up a privacy fence to block off your backyard.

If you talk to your neighbors about what your business is doing, you shouldn't have many problems. Realize, though, that by going public about your program, you may run into some opposition from neighbors who might otherwise have been unaware of your business. If you are concerned about this, you can choose not to be so public with your neighbors. In most cases, however, neighbors are happy to have a provider close by. Invite your neighbors to an open house when you are getting started. Distribute your business cards and flyers and tell them what openings you have. Throw an Easter egg hunt, Halloween party, Labor Day picnic, "Good Neighbor Day" party, or holiday party for the children and your neighbors. Participate in any block party and talk about your business. Ask neighbors to talk to you first if they have any questions or concerns about what you are doing. Happy neighbors can help you market your program through positive word of mouth.

A special problem can exist for providers who rent or live in a housing development run by a homeowners association. Local and state laws govern the rights of renters or homeowners in these situations. In many areas, landlords or housing covenants can prohibit the operation of any business, including family child care programs. If you face opposition from associations or zoning laws, use the arguments described in this chapter. Try to point out that your particular business doesn't really create any serious problems for others. Ask your family child care association to help you lobby for changes to restrictive laws affecting providers. For more information, see the *Family Child Care Legal and Insurance Guide*.

When to Say No to Enrolling a Child

It may seem strange to say this in a book about marketing your program and building enrollment, but there are times when you should *not* enroll a child. Your goal as a business is to provide a quality service to parents and children. If your service doesn't fit a particular child or family well, you will be doing everyone a favor by not signing a contract with that parent. If you enroll a child knowing there are potential problems, and if you end up terminating care later under a cloud of bad feelings, you, the parent, and the child will all be dissatisfied. You want to avoid short-term relationships with enrolled families. To prevent negative word of mouth, don't be afraid to say no before care begins.

What clues might indicate a provider-family mismatch? There are no absolutes, but here are a few signs:

- The parent refuses to give you the name of a previous caregiver as a reference.
- The child seems out of control. (Note: Under the ADA, providers may not discriminate against children with disabilities. See page 33 for further discussion about the ADA.)
- The parent does not seem interested in her own child or the kind of care you say you will be offering.
- The parent does not treat you with respect or is not flexible about adapting to your program.
- The parent seems uncomfortable with your rates or payment policies.
- The parent wants you to make special accommodations for him or his child that you are uncomfortable with.

Not every provider will react the same way to every parent. It pays, however, to trust your feelings about the parent and child. Many providers offer a two-week trial period to help sort out any potential conflicts or mismatches; the parent or the provider can terminate service without notice during this trial period.

If you make the decision not to enroll a child, how do you say no to the parent? Do not be negative or critical about either the child or the parent. Such criticism will only backfire when the parent talks to someone else about you. The best thing to say is, "I don't feel that this is the best place for your child at this time." A neutral statement such as this does not place blame, and it allows the parent to back out gracefully. Do not elaborate or offer any further explanation for your decision. You make many decisions in your business based on your personal feelings, and this is one more example. You may want to refer the parent to the local CCR&R agency, family child care association, or child care regulatory office for help in finding another provider. These actions may ease the parent's mind after your refusal.

Many providers find saying no to parents difficult. Oftentimes providers try to avoid a direct confrontation with a parent by saying, "I interviewed some parents earlier this week, and I'm waiting to hear back from them about filling my opening. After I talk to them in the next few days, I'll let you know if I still have an opening." In general, I don't think this is a good strategy to use with parents. First, it's not truthful—and that's unprofessional. Second, if a parent later sees that you still have an ad on Craigslist or an opening with the local CCR&R agency, she may conclude that you lied to her. This may lead her to believe that you discriminated against her in some way, and she may complain to your licensor. At the very least, the parent will not feel good about you, and she will likely spread bad (not good) word of mouth about your program.

Child Care Flyer

When parents are looking for child care, they may not know what questions to ask a provider. They may also need help keeping track of all the programs they contacted. To help the parents remember your program, prepare a simple "Choosing Child Care Checklist" flyer. See appendix F for an example.

You may want to use copies of flyers already developed by your local CCR&R agency, your local family child care association, or the National Association for Family Child Care (NAFCC). (See the brochure *Why Choose Nationally Accredited Family Child Care?* on the NAFCC website, for example.) Appendix M has more information on how to contact these organizations. If you use a flyer developed by someone else, put your name and phone number on it before you distribute it.

Send copies of your flyer (by mail or e-mail) to parents when they call, or give them one when they come for an interview. Encourage parents to compare your program with others. Refer to the contents of the flyer to point out the benefits of your program. By doing so, you help parents think about what they need to look for in a child care program, and you provide a service that will make potential customers remember you.

Photo Album and Scrapbook

When parents come to your home for an interview, they usually will not have time to see all your program has to offer. Assemble a photo album or scrapbook (both are cheaper than making a video, although some providers do use videos) for parents to thumb through during the interview process or when you get busy or are interrupted. You can refer to the album as you describe your program. (The children in your care may also enjoy looking at your photo album and scrapbook. They will enjoy reflecting on past group activities and experiences and remembering friends who have left.)

Because most providers will show parents their photo album, take steps to make yours stand out. Photos don't clearly identify the benefits of your program by themselves. Take the time to add captions to some of the photos (every five or ten) that explain the benefits they illustrate:

- "Cleaning up after lunch: the children are learning responsibility."
- "Holiday party: the children love singing for their parents."
- "Field trip to a local park: the children are learning about nature."
- "Learning activity: the children are reading/sharing/counting/dancing/ singing."

See appendix E, "Skills Children Learn in Family Child Care," for more information on how to identify what children are learning. You may want to make copies of this skills list and give it to parents. When you show photos of children learning, you communicate the value of your program to parents.

A scrapbook need not contain only photos; it can include other information as well:

- accreditation, training, and educational credentials
- past parent evaluations or references
- descriptions of special activities
- newspaper stories about your program
- a copy of your license
- a copy of your business flyer
- certificates and awards
- information about special or important visitors, such as an elected official, licensing worker, or puppeteer (have visitors sign a guest list or book)
- thank-you notes and cards from current and past clients

Be sure to get written permission from parents before including any photos of their children in your photo album or scrapbook.

Enrollment Packet

An enrollment packet is a compilation of forms and information for parents who are about to enroll their child in your program. This is easier to put together than you might think. Such a packet doesn't need to look slick, just neat and organized. You can distribute your packet at the end of an interview or mail it to parents a week before the first day of care. Your packet might include the following:

- enrollment forms, such as a contract (indicating your hours and rates), medical consent forms, medical information forms, and policies (such as for discipline guidance, sickness, meals, and field trips)
- a description of your services and special program activities or events
- a copy of your license or registration
- a summary of your hours and days closed (such as holidays, vacations, or professional days)
- several copies of your business card

- the latest copy of your newsletter

- a copy of your business flyer

- your résumé

- a description of your child caring philosophy

- newspaper articles or other information about your program

- a flyer describing the benefits of family child care (your local CCR&R agency might have one you can use; see appendix M for information on how to contact this organization)

Your enrollment packet can look professional without being expensive. Purchase folders with pockets for flyers and business cards. Don't give out an enrollment packet unless a parent is signing up. It's too expensive to give a packet to everyone who calls. Before an interview, send only your business flyer to those who call.

Improve Your Professional Credentials

Providing high-quality child care for young children of different ages and with different needs takes skill, and this skill requires training and experience. Studies indicate that training in child development is more important than experience with children when measuring high-quality care. That's why providers should do everything they can to improve their education credentials. In an increasingly competitive market, parents will be looking for objective standards of quality to help them choose a child care program. Accomplishments in the field of education will be even more important to many parents in the future.

Although there is no single educational achievement that all providers should attain, here are some professional development credentials to explore:

- The National Association for Family Child Care (NAFCC) offers an accreditation program designed to promote and recognize high-quality, professional family child care. The program requires training, a self-study process, and a home visit by an observer. For contact information about this program, see the NAFCC listing in appendix M.

- The Council for Professional Recognition developed the Child Development Associate (CDA) credential to improve the quality of child care. This is an individual credential acquired through a non–college degree course of study. Providers must complete 120 hours of training in a variety of areas through technical colleges, CCR&R agencies, and workshops sponsored by other organizations. For further information, see the Council for Professional Recognition listing in appendix M.

- Providers may want to obtain a postsecondary degree in child development, elementary education, early childhood education, or school-age care. Many colleges and universities offer two- or four-year programs. Providers who have postsecondary degrees in other fields that are relevant to children, such as nursing, general education, or foreign languages, can use these qualifications to improve the quality of care they offer. They should list these degrees as a benefit when describing their program. The types of postsecondary degrees offered by colleges and universities vary greatly by state and institution. Contact a local education institution for information about the most appropriate course of study for you. Also check to see if your government child care subsidy agency reimburses providers at a higher rate if they earn a postsecondary degree.

- Increasingly, providers are receiving education degrees online. If you have access to the Internet, you may want to explore this option. The NAFCC and the National Association of Child Care Resource and Referral Agencies (NACCRRA) both offer online classes and webinars for family child care providers.

- The Quality Rating and Improvement System (QRIS) is a national movement to increase the quality of child care by using rating systems and improvement strategies to elevate the quality of care at the state level. Many states have implemented their own QRIS programs, often with a four-star rating system. You should participate in this program—if one is available—and educate parents on how your rating reflects how well you meet standards for high-quality care. See appendix M for a link to the QRIS program in your state.

- Some states have special training projects and credential programs available for family child care providers. Contact your local CCR&R agency for further information about what is available in your area.

- Redleaf Press publishes the *Go Green Rating Scale for Early Childhood Settings,* which offers a comprehensive, research-based set of standards you can use to measure the environmental health of your program. See appendix M, "Additional Resources," for more information.

- Because our society is a multicultural community and potential customers come from increasingly diverse backgrounds, plan to attend workshops to learn about different cultures so all of your customers feel comfortable in your program. Get to know other providers from different cultures, and ask them for advice. The more you know about children's backgrounds, the better you'll be able to help all children learn.

- Local training opportunities are often available to providers. Take as many early childhood development and early care and education trainings as possible. Many organizations offer such training: CCR&R agencies, Child and Adult Care Food Program (CACFP) sponsors, community colleges, family child care associations, and universities. Contact your local CCR&R agency for further information.

- Life experience is a credential. Although studies show that training is more important than experience in defining high-quality care, providers should not lose sight of the fact that experience can make a difference. A mother or grandmother who has raised her own children and grandchildren can certainly claim knowledge about what it takes to be a caregiver. Life experiences combined with additional training and certification create a powerful way to compete.

Use your education and life experiences to help market your program. Display your credentials to prospective parents (on your bulletin board and in your newsletters, website, flyers, and contract) and keep current clients informed of all new training classes and workshops you attend. Use every opportunity to show parents how your knowledge and skills help you do a better job of teaching their child.

Display Your Credentials

Parents look for signs of high quality in their child's provider and program. Important measures of this quality are educational credentials and other accomplishments and achievements. Because regulations vary so much from state to state, parents have little guidance from objective sources about whether your program is high quality. Displaying your training credentials is an important way to communicate high quality. You should take every opportunity to inform parents about your credentials, which may include some of the following:

- a CDA credential
- accreditation through the NAFCC Accreditation program
- a degree in child development or other child care field from a college or university
- a certificate showing your ranking in your state's QRIS
- classes in child development taken at local educational institutions
- a degree in nursing, home economics, elementary education, or other fields that are relevant to the care of children
- community awards
- awards from local and state family child care associations
- a child care license or registration certificate
- experience as an officer or board member of a family child care association
- participation at state or national child care conferences, such as the NAFCC conference, Quality Care for Children conference, or National Association for the Education of Young Children (NAEYC) conference
- your status as a Food Program participant
- a certificate of attendance at a workshop sponsored by the Food Program, CCR&R agency, or family child care association
- your experience as a parent of four children and a grandparent of two
- positive stories about your program in a local newspaper

Display notices of these achievements on your bulletin board for prospective parents to see. List accreditations and degrees on your business cards and flyers. Announce new accomplishments in your newsletter and website. Put copies of your credentials in your photo album or scrapbook and in your enrollment packet. Frame your important credentials and permanently display them on your wall.

Offer a Special Service

With the growing number of child care programs for parents to choose from, it will become increasingly difficult to get parents to notice you. One way to stand out from the competition is to offer a unique service for parents and their children. Think of any particular skill or interest you might have that could translate into a new service. Below are some examples of special services you might offer:

- Offer a summer activity program that involves extended field trips, ball games, swimming, camping, boating, gardening, or community art projects.
- Contact your local 4-H club to see if your program can collaborate with its activities.
- Plant a community garden in your backyard with your clients and their children. Use the garden to teach the children about plants and nutrition. Give them vegetables and herbs to take home.
- Offer overnight care for special days (for example, Valentine's Day or Mother's Day) or when parents go to a play or movie, or go bowling.
- Cook an occasional evening meal-to-go for parents to take home when they pick up their children. Parents can order their meal in advance.
- Bring in a gymnastics or ballet instructor to teach the children so parents spend less time driving to these lessons.
- Provide haircuts for children.
- Offer music lessons.
- Take children to organized T-ball activities.
- Stay open late one day a week to give parents time to run errands.

- Offer parenting classes on evenings or weekends on topics you feel qualified to teach. Or bring in a professional trainer to teach CPR or first aid.

- Take children to activities sponsored by local religious organizations.

- Buy a caged animal (such as a guinea pig or mouse) and teach the children how to care for and raise it. The animal could become your business mascot.

- Specialize your offerings by providing only school-age care.

- Have your older children offer to babysit on evenings and weekends for your clients.

- Specialize your offerings by providing care only for children with special needs. If you do this, you could focus your marketing efforts on community organizations that serve parents of children who have special needs.

- Throw a family picnic in the summer so families can meet one another.

- In December, provide evening care so parents can do their holiday shopping. Advertise this service to the friends of current clients and others. December is a time when parents start to think about making new child care arrangements. One provider offered a "parent co-op," where she stayed open until 10:00 p.m. the four Fridays between Thanksgiving and Christmas. Parents who brought their child to the program during one of these evenings had to work one of the other three Friday evenings. The provider cooked dinner, and the parent cared for the children. The parents appreciated the three evenings they could shop, and the provider reported that each parent gained a new understanding of group child care.

If you begin offering a special service, try to identify new places to market the service to parents. For instance, if you begin offering piano lessons, you can advertise at music schools or talk with music teachers at local elementary schools. If you want to attract more children with special needs, approach the local organizations that serve such children and begin advertising there. If you are offering school-age care, approach your local elementary schools to see if you can distribute your business flyers.

Before offering any special service, you may want to survey your current clients to gauge their level of interest. List the special services you are considering, and ask parents whether they are very likely, somewhat likely, or not at all likely to use each service. You can attach surveys to payment receipts or hand them out at pickup time. Even if your current clients are not interested in your ideas, you may still want to offer the services to attract new clients.

Family child care providers can meet some parent needs more effectively than child care centers. Evening, weekend, and rotating-shift care are some specific examples. This kind of care is fairly expensive for centers to provide because of the high overhead cost of a building and the uncertain cost of appropriate staffing. Family child care programs can provide this type of care much more easily. Many providers, however, choose not to offer this type of care because of the long hours and the disruptions it might cause with their own family. There is definitely a demand for this special service, and providers who choose to offer it are likely to be successful.

Many providers may conclude that they don't have the time or energy to offer special services. It's okay to acknowledge that you already have enough to do! For example, you may decide to offer a special service only to find that the added work means you need extra help to care for the children. Don't allow the quality of your regular care to suffer because of a special service. But before rejecting the idea of offering a special service, think about what it would mean for you and your family to be able to do it. You may find that this can be a source of extra money that will more than pay for your extra work. Parents will often pay significantly more for a special service. Some providers may decide to include some special services as a part of their regular offerings and promote them as additional benefits to keep current parents and attract new ones.

Become a Community Volunteer

Volunteering for a community organization may seem unrealistic—particularly because most family child care providers work very long hours—but it's something you may want to consider. Volunteering for local community organizations that serve children (such as a church nursery, the children's reading room in the public library, a women's shelter, or a food pantry) can be a way to introduce yourself to prospective clients in a setting that reflects well on you. You may be able to conduct volunteer work in the evenings or on weekends.

Halloween

Why is Halloween a special day for many family child care providers? It is the one day of the year that potential clients are knocking on your door! Take advantage of this opportunity to advertise your business:

- Put in your window a sign that can be read from the street telling parents about your business ("Preschool Opening").

- Invite trick-or-treaters and their parents into your home for cocoa, apple cider, or coffee. If your children's play area is visible from the entryway, turn on the lights in the room so everyone can see what a fun space you have for children. Don't be shy about showing off your space.

- Give parents your business flyer, business card, and a keepsake (see page 86). Encourage them to tell others about your business.

- Put your business card and keepsake into the child's candy bag. The parents will find it later. One provider sent me a sample of the business cards she gives out on Halloween. On the card she had taped two crayons that matched the colors on her card. Other providers give out children's toothbrushes, toothpaste, or sugar-free suckers or candy along with their business cards. Such Halloween goodies clearly communicate your concern for children's health and will attract parents' attention.

CHAPTER 4

Marketing to Current Clients

Keeping your current customers satisfied is one of the first goals for any marketing plan. You want current customers to stay with you as long as possible because it is far cheaper to keep them happy than it is to attract new customers. Don't ever take it for granted that your clients are completely satisfied. Continue to talk to them about what they need. Learn to be a good listener. Ask them how their child likes your care. Use a contract update or written evaluation as an opportunity to listen. Keep trying to improve the quality of your program. If parents are happy, they will probably tell others and give you a favorable review. Parents who are unhappy and share negative impressions can hurt your program.

You can market to current clients in a variety of ways, some of which are described in this chapter. Use these ideas to convey to families that the child care service they are receiving is worthwhile. You may want to build loyalty by giving rewards to parents who stay with you for an extended period of time. For example, you could offer a free evening (or day) of care for every six months of enrollment.

Ask parents to be more involved in your program by becoming volunteers. Parents can read to children, help out on field trips, prepare activities at their own home and bring them over, make phone calls to remind other parents of upcoming events, copy and mail your newsletter, or help build playground equipment. Some providers ask clients to fill out a parent volunteer checklist at the time of enrollment to indicate how they might support their program. Some parents will have special skills, such as a background in accounting, law, advertising, or marketing. If necessary, you could barter care in exchange for some of this help.

Keep the lines of communication open with your current clients. Greet them each day with a smile. Always have information to share at drop-off and pickup times. At drop-off, you might say, "Today we will be playing outside in the sand, where Joshua will learn about measuring and sharing." In the evening, you might say, "Joshua had a lot of fun filling up pails with sand, and he spent time playing with Cindy and Velissa." Parents are more likely to leave a child care program because of poor communication than because of high rates.

Do not let conflicts over your contract and policies destroy your relationship with current clients. Enforce your rules consistently and review them regularly with your clients. When you will have an opening, let your current clients know immediately by writing them a note. Be direct about asking them to share the news. You might offer a finder's fee, send flowers, or cook supper for a successful referral. Also consider using other tools to help you keep in touch with parents, such as Facebook (see chapter 7), your website, a bulletin board, or a newsletter. In your efforts to keep clients happy, never underestimate the value of simply listening and talking to your current clients every day.

Helping New Clients Feel Comfortable

Generally, new clients are the most likely to drop out of your program six to eight weeks after enrollment. It's not uncommon for parents and children to feel uneasy during their first few days or weeks in child care. You can help make this transition period go smoothly if you take steps to reassure both the parent and the child. Here are some ways to help your new clients feel more comfortable:

- Shortly after a parent signs up, call the parent or send a note to thank him for enrolling his child in your program.

- Before the first day of enrollment, send a note to both the parent and the child welcoming them to your program. Enclose a photograph of you and the children in your care. You may want to include this photo in your enrollment packet as well.

- Encourage the parent to create a voice recording on her home computer. Ask her to read, sing, or talk to her child on the recording. Parents can use online resources, such as Odeo (www.odeo.com) or Audacity (http://audacity.sourceforge.net), or computer programs, such as the Windows Sound Recorder (on a PC) or Garageband (on a Mac). The parents can then e-mail the recording to you as an MP3 file. Play the recording for the child to help calm her during the early weeks.

- Ask the parent to bring in family pictures that can be displayed for the child to see.

- Have the child bring a favorite toy or blanket from home.

- If practical, ask the family to bring their household pet for the child to share with the other children.

- Create a personal space (a cubby or other special area) for the child, and label it with his name to help him feel more safe and secure.

- Have someone take a picture of you and the child playing with the other children, and give it to the parent for him to post at his workplace. Take pictures (or a video) of the child's first days in your program and place them in a scrapbook to share with the family.

- Ask the parent if she would like you to call her (or e-mail her or text her) at work and let her know how her child is doing. As another option, invite her to call you to check in.

- Make a point of communicating closely with the parent by asking him how things are going for him and the child during the first few weeks.

- Share with the parent that it can take up to two weeks for a child to feel comfortable enough to have an easy transition when the parent leaves.

- Invite the parent to call anytime she needs assurance that her child is adjusting well and feeling comfortable.

- Invite the parent to drop in at will if he needs assurance that his child's day is going smoothly or the care is what he expects.

- If a lot of time has passed between the time of the enrollment interview and the child's first day of care, suggest a ten- to fifteen-minute visit one or two days before the child begins attending. Doing so will help reintroduce the child to you and the program.

All of these steps can help you quickly earn the trust of parents and set the stage for a long-lasting relationship.

Finder's Fee

One of the first steps you should take to promote your business is to offer current parents in your program a finder's fee, which is a financial incentive for referring new clients to your program who then enroll their child. You might say to a current client, "If you refer a new family to my program and I enroll the family, I will give you a finder's fee after the new parent has paid me for a month of child care." Don't pay a finder's fee until the new child has been enrolled for at least one month and the arrangement appears likely to last.

I've found that most providers set their finder's fee between twenty-five and fifty dollars. If you are able to fill your spaces with a twenty-five-dollar finder's fee, then don't offer a higher amount. If you are having trouble filling spaces with your twenty-five-dollar fee, raise it. During a recession, many parents will appreciate a higher finder's fee. When thinking about setting a finder's fee for the first time, consider how long enrolled children will stay in your program: One year? Two years? Longer? This usually means tens of thousands of dollars of tuition! Paying a hundred-dollar finder's fee certainly isn't expensive when viewed in this light. The finder's fee amount that works best for providers varies considerably across the country. Find out what other child care homes and centers in your area offer as a finder's fee so you can compete.

You can add whatever terms you want to your finder's fee. You can put a time limit on the fee or offer a fee only for hard-to-fill openings (such as preschool care). Consider offering a finder's fee to clients who have left your program, parents who contacted you but didn't enroll, and friends, neighbors, or anyone else who could spread the word about your program.

Rather than cash, some providers offer parents a free weekend of care or a week of free care for every successful referral. Other providers offer gift cards to local restaurants and businesses, such as Baby Gap, Babies"R"Us, Barnes and Noble, Chuck E. Cheese's, and so on. The fee can be anything you, or the parent, want! If you give parents cash or gift cards as a finder's fee, you can deduct the amount as a business expense. If you give parents free child care, your business income will be lower, and therefore your taxes will be lower. You can't deduct the value of the care you give away.

Offering a finder's fee is a low-cost, no-lose way to promote your program. Unlike paid advertising, you will pay out of pocket only after you've enrolled a new family and received the income of at least a month's worth of child care. In addition, a finder's fee encourages current clients to spread good word of mouth about your program without any cost to you. Also, current clients will be selective about their referrals because they will want the new child to be compatible with their own child. Give your business cards to parents so they can pass them out to prospective clients.

Some providers choose not to offer a finder's fee because they feel it is unprofessional or it makes them appear desperate to parents. These providers might believe that giving away any of their time will cause clients to put a lower value on their services. Often these providers simply send parents a thank-you card for the referral. In my opinion, there is nothing desperate or unprofessional about offering a finder's fee. Other businesses regularly offer deals to their customers without complaint. Make your own decision about whether a finder's fee is a good idea for your program. If you don't feel comfortable offering a finder's fee, don't do it. But remember, paying to fill a space in your program is cheaper than almost any other type of advertising you can do.

Bulletin Board

Using a bulletin board is a good way to communicate with current parents. Place the bulletin board where parents will easily see it each morning and evening. Post weekly menus; news of incoming or outgoing parents, upcoming field trips, and upcoming birthdays; current newspaper or magazine articles about child care or child development; your license; your training credentials; news of local child care advocacy efforts; announcements of new policies; and reminders of when fees are due. You can also post photos of the children (with parents' permission), the parents (with their permission), or any recent special event. Use the bulletin board to share daily activities and describe to parents what skills the children are learning; see appendix E, "Skills Children Learn in Family Child Care," for ideas. If you receive letters and photos from former clients or children, post those as well.

Periodically change the content of your bulletin board to keep it current. Throw out old news. Decorate it for upcoming holidays and events. Parents will notice your bulletin board more often if you constantly add and remove items. Your bulletin board should be a source of news and information about what parents can expect from you. It is a professional way to communicate with parents because it can be used to continually educate them about the benefits of your program. The more parents understand what you do for their child, the more they will value your service.

Newsletter

Keep in touch with parents by sending them a regular newsletter. The newsletter can contain all kinds of information:

- weekly menus
- children's artwork
- short descriptions of what the children are learning
- parenting tips (from magazine or newspaper articles)
- new policies
- news of any state child care advocacy efforts by your local family child care association or other child care agency
- introductions of new children and farewells to those moving on
- current articles from newspapers or magazines about child care issues (with permission to excerpt from the publisher)
- your commentary on stories in the news
- upcoming birthdays and anniversaries
- reminders of when payments are due
- upcoming activities and special events

Your newsletter can be produced on a computer using a variety of typestyles and scanned-in photos. If you don't have a computer, print your newsletter by hand.

You can find newsletter templates and helpful links at the Free Newsletter Templates website (www.freenewsletter-templates.com). To add special touches, use the clip art found in many software programs or reproduce photographs on a copier and place them in your newsletter. Search for free clip art online with your search engine— such as Google or Bing; here are a few websites I've found: Clipart (www.pppst .com/clipart.html), Teacher Files (www.teacherfiles.com/clip_art.htm), School Clip Art (www.school-clip-art.com). Consider using a different color of paper for each issue of your newsletter. You could also add color with a marker or simply print each issue in color with a color printer. If your business has a logo or tagline, put it at the top of each issue. Don't worry about trying to produce a fancy newsletter. The most important thing is for your newsletter to look clean and interesting and be readable.

Many providers produce their newsletter once a month, but you can decide whether you want to send one out more or less often. Pick a schedule that is comfortable for you. It might be a good idea to send your newsletter quarterly at first and then switch to monthly as you can, rather than starting with an ambitious schedule and then failing to meet your own deadlines.

Send your newsletter to all current and past clients, parents who called or visited your program but did not enroll their child, any parents on your waiting list, and your friends. Everyone who receives your newsletter can help you promote your business through good word of mouth. To save money and to use less paper, you can distribute your newsletter through e-mail as a PDF document. You can find simple instructions on how to create a PDF file on this website: http://tinyurl .com/7yu4yrm.

Several commercial parent newsletters are available for providers. They include a variety of activities parents can do with their children. You can pass on copies of these monthly newsletters to your clients or use some of the articles in your own newsletter. Two such newsletters are *Parent Pages Newsletter* (www.parentpagesnews .com) and *Growing Together* (http://growingchild.com/GrowingTogether.html).

Birthday and Holiday Cards

Everyone likes receiving birthday and holiday cards. Mail cards to children in your care, as well as to their parents. Send holiday cards (for Christmas, Kwanzaa, Rosh Hashanah, Ramadan, and so on) as long as you know that the family celebrates the particular holiday. When a child starts attending your program, ask the parents what holidays they celebrate at home. Ask them for appropriate ways to recognize holidays in your program. Let parents know that you want to share as much of each child's culture in your program as possible. List the children's birthdays in your newsletter and on your bulletin board so all parents can congratulate the child. Send a card when a client has or adopts a new child. If a child or a child's family member is in the hospital, send a get-well card. Send a card when a parent does something unusually nice for you or your program. You may also want to send cards for Mother's Day, Father's Day, Valentine's Day, and New Year's Day.

Other Communication

We communicate not only by what we say but also by how we say it. Most providers have no trouble communicating through speech, so special attention needs to be paid to other communication skills. Written documents can make remembering important information easier for parents. They also create more legitimacy for your business. Parents are less likely to argue with you if you set out your rules in clear prose. When you want to change a rule or make an announcement, put it in writing and give it to parents. Tell parents you will be happy to answer any questions they might have. Here are some other tips:

- Write regular notes to parents describing their child's activities or eating and sleeping patterns. For infants and toddlers, make daily notes. Always find something positive to say about the child. Slip notes in with the child's belongings, pin them to her clothing, or hand them directly to parents.

- Take a picture of a new child playing with the other children. E-mail it to the parents at work. Parents may want to post the photograph at their desk where coworkers (and potential new clients) may see it.

- If you plan to change any rule in your program, particularly a rule dealing with money or your hours, give parents at least a month's notice. Any change to a written contract must be made in writing.

- Make copies of newspaper or magazine articles on parenting or child care issues and give them to parents. Post articles about parenting or child care issues on your bulletin board. Ask parents if they can recommend a helpful article or book for you to share with the other parents in the program.

- Post pictures of new families on your bulletin board to welcome them to your program.

- Give parents a receipt each time they pay you and a summary receipt at the end of the year. Doing so is a sign of professionalism. It communicates to parents that you are running a well-organized business that treats its customers with respect.

- Dress appropriately. The way you dress is an important form of nonverbal communication. You want to look professional but not overdressed. Your clothing should be casual and neat. Consider your families to be company, and dress as if a casual friend were about to arrive. If you get messy during the day, clean up before the parents arrive. Hang a special apron or smock by the front door to put on if your clothes are messy and parents stop by unexpectedly. Your customers' children should look clean at the end of the day as well. If they have dirty faces or hands, parents may wonder if their child is receiving enough of your attention.

Celebrations

Invite the children in your care and their parents to a party at your home at least once a year. Having a festive gathering gives you an opportunity to interact with clients at a time that is less stressful than the pickup and drop-off times during the workweek. During the party, share some of the positive things that the children are learning, have the children sing songs, or just have a good time. Your party could celebrate a holiday (such as Christmas, Kwanzaa, Hanukkah, Ramadan, Chinese New Year, Rosh Hashanah, Independence Day, or Memorial Day) or a season (such as a backyard gathering in the summer). If you celebrate a religious holiday, make sure your clients also celebrate it. You could celebrate Grandparents Day and invite all grandparents to a party. Talk to your families about what occasions they celebrate and try to incorporate their traditions into your program.

If you have been in business for a number of years, consider having an anniversary party to celebrate the life of your program. Invite past clients as well. Take pictures of the event and put them in your newsletter, on your website, on Facebook, on the bulletin board, or in your photo album. Send an announcement about your anniversary (and a follow-up photo) for the local media to cover. See page 137 for more information about generating media publicity.

Whether you are celebrating a special event or holiday or are just throwing a party, invite current, former, and prospective clients. You may even want to invite neighbors and friends to help spread the good news about your program. One provider in Texas has a summer barbecue every year and invites current, former, and prospective clients. Last year, more than 150 people attended! This is a marvelous way to promote a program. It allows parents and children to connect with and support one another. It shows current parents that your program is a good place for their children because you create a long-term extended-family environment for them. A celebration also gives you an opportunity to remind former clients that you are trying to fill openings (offer a finder's fee!), and it sends the message to everyone involved that your service to children is valued and important.

Some child care providers offer parents a "Parents' Night Out." The provider offers a free evening of child care so the parents can go holiday shopping. This is something that single parents especially appreciate. One provider I know offers a free evening of care in exchange for help when she offers a free evening of care for another parent. The provider says that she does this so the parent can get a better idea of what it's like caring for multiple children. She says that afterward the parent usually has a new appreciation for the work she does!

Another provider offers a "Mom's Night Out" for mothers of the children in her program. She invites them to a formal dinner at her home (the dads stay home with the children). Her own teenage children serve the food and, earlier in the day, the child care children prepare the dessert. This activity helps the provider bond with the mothers, who look forward to the dinner.

Contract and Policies Update

Family child care providers should have written contracts and policies that they use with their customers to operate their business. Your contract should contain all matters dealing with your fees and hours of operation; these are the things you can enforce in court. Your policies should contain everything else about how you will deliver your services, including your discipline, feeding, and sickness policies. You enforce your policies, ultimately, by terminating your contract.

Your contract and policies are your primary tools for communicating responsibilities and expectations to parents. Review your contract and policies with parents at least once a year to make sure everyone understands their roles. Ask parents to explain what each policy and contract term means to them. If their explanation is different from your understanding, change the wording to reflect your intent. If a policy is outdated and no longer relevant, delete it. Add new policies as necessary. Include only those policies you will enforce. For more ideas, ask other providers what they include in their contract and policies (see page 170 for a warning about price fixing). The goals of your review are to keep current clients informed and happy and to reduce the likelihood of misunderstandings.

Discuss the progress of each child with parents at least monthly. At these parent conferences, share information about the child's interests and progress. At least once a year, distribute a parent evaluation. If you don't use a written evaluation, use this opportunity to ask the parents general questions:

- "How are things going for you and your child? Do you have any concerns?"
- "Are there any other services you would like me to offer?"
- "Can you think of ways that I could advertise my program to attract new clients?"

Regularly asking these questions helps you stay in touch with what clients are thinking. It will help you keep current clients enrolled and give you insight into finding new ones. For examples of contracts and policies and an explanation of how they are different, see *Family Child Care Contracts and Policies* (published by Redleaf Press).

Curriculum

An increasing number of family child care providers are using a curriculum to help children learn. A curriculum can create a more structured learning environment for your program. Parents sometimes feel more confident that their child is learning if you can show them your curriculum. A curriculum can be commercially produced, or it can be something you develop yourself. Here are a couple of examples of family child care curricula:

- *Family Child Care Curriculum* by Sharon Woodward (published by Redleaf Press)
- *The Creative Curriculum for Family Child Care* by Diane Trister Dodge, Sherrie Rudick, and Laura Colker (published by Teaching Strategies)

Use your curriculum to promote your program. Tell parents, "I use the XXX curriculum, which is designed to help your child learn about letters, numbers, and more. I will keep you informed about how well your child is doing with this curriculum." Or you might say, "I pay close attention to the individual needs of each child. Then I design my own curriculum to help your child learn. I've been using my own child-centered curriculum for many years and have found that children respond very positively to my approach."

Whether your curriculum is highly structured or informal, emphasize to parents how your curriculum will help their child learn.

Video

Parents often do not have a complete picture of what goes on in your program every day. Some providers periodically record videos of their day to help educate their clients. You can use videos to show parents how you encourage reading, physical development, playing skills, helping skills, counting, and toothbrushing. Shoot a video of special events (birthday or holiday parties) or record a typical morning or afternoon activity. For new clients, consider focusing on their child for a day. If you have older children, ask them to help shoot a video, or have them direct the entire video themselves. Get written permission from parents before recording any video (see appendix K, "Photo, Voice, Website, Facebook, and Video Permission Form"). If you don't own a video camera, borrow one from a friend or customer, or rent one. Many smartphones allow you to record videos and play them back on a computer or television.

Consider playing the videos as parents are dropping off or picking up their children. Doing so allows parents to catch a few additional glimpses of your program in operation. You can offer to burn a DVD for parents who want to see more. By making the video available, you send the message that you want clients to learn more about your program. Even if some clients don't watch the video, they will still feel reassured that you care. The more parents see what you are doing with the children, the more they will appreciate your program.

Some providers may want to make a more professional-looking video for prospective clients. There are many easy-to-use editing programs that allow you to make and edit very professional-looking videos on a personal computer or tablet. You can burn the video onto DVDs, which are very inexpensive. Keep your video short: ten to fifteen minutes is enough. Display your business name and phone number on both the DVD and the DVD case. Be sure to get written permission from the parents of any children in the video (see appendix K, "Photo, Voice, Website, Facebook, and Video Permission Form"). Give a DVD to parents at parent interviews or mail one to interested callers. You could also post your video on YouTube and allow only parents in your program to see it.

Evaluations

To help you stay on top of what current clients are thinking about your program, ask them to fill out an evaluation form once a year. Your evaluation should be simple and include some of these key questions:

- What do you like best about my program?
- What could I do to improve my program?
- Do you have any other comments or suggestions?

Here are some additional evaluation questions you may want to include:

- What special services are you interested in that I could offer?
- What does your child say about being here?
- What would you say about my program to another parent?

You may want to distribute your evaluation form when you distribute your contract and policies for review. See appendix J for a sample evaluation form.

When clients are leaving your care, ask them if you can use their name as a reference for prospective clients or quote them in your marketing efforts, such as in a business flyer. Always ask clients who are leaving your program to fill out an evaluation. In this situation add this question to your regular evaluation form:

- Will you recommend my program to other parents? Why or why not?

Put positive evaluations in a scrapbook or photo album so new clients can see these written references.

Read all evaluations carefully. Don't worry if you receive some negative feedback; you can't please everyone. If a suggestion is impractical (such as "stay open till 10:00 p.m. for drop-in care"), simply tell parents you can't meet this need. If the suggestion is a reasonable one, try to do it. Thank parents for their suggestions, compliments, and criticisms. Tell parents what action will be taken to address their complaints. If practical, ask parents to monitor your follow-up to their concerns. Another good way to respond to client suggestions is to write a note in your newsletter or post a response on your bulletin board.

Look closely at the words parents use to describe the positive aspects of your program.

- "The individual attention you provide to meet Sally's needs is wonderful."
- "Akimi loves to play with all your fun toys."
- "I appreciate your flexible hours, especially your willingness to accommodate my work schedule during busy seasons."

Positive comments from clients will probably be given in the form of benefits (see chapter 2). Try to use these phrases in your discussions with prospective clients. For example, say, "Parents in my program tell me they appreciate the individual attention I give their children and my flexible hours."

Many parents will be reluctant to express any dissatisfaction with your child care program because they don't want to offend you. If they are frustrated, however, they might say negative things to others about your program, whether you know about their dissatisfaction or not. To reduce this possibility, encourage parents to express their frustrations directly to you. Ask them how things are going on a regular basis, and ask for their ideas about how you could improve your program. Don't rely on written evaluations as your only source of feedback from clients.

If you are sensitive to negative feedback, talk about your feelings with your spouse or a friend. Never complain to a customer about another customer's criticism of you. Do not be quick to terminate a client who voices criticism. Try to learn to accept criticism without feeling personally attacked. Once you deal with criticism by making a change (or by deciding not to change), put it behind you. Let it go, and enjoy the new day. See my book *Family Child Care Contracts and Policies* for a discussion of how to communicate and negotiate with clients.

Some parents will be reluctant to give criticism face-to-face. To encourage communication, some providers use a suggestion box so parents can give feedback anonymously throughout the year. You can prepare a suggestion form for parents to fill out that is similar to the evaluation form described earlier. Handle suggestions from a suggestion box in the same way you handle other feedback. Be reassured that most criticism from parents is constructive because they want your business to succeed too.

Child and Dependent Care Assistance Plans

You should do anything you can to make it financially more attractive for parents to continue coming to your program. For example, you should make sure that all parents participate in a dependent care assistance plan if their employers offer one. This employer benefit plan allows parents to set aside a portion of their salary up to a certain limit ($5,000 for a married couple in 2012) to be spent on child care. The amount set aside is not subject to any federal or state income taxes. This represents a substantial tax savings for many families and is usually more beneficial than the child care tax credit. These plans are also known as "cafeteria plans," "flexible benefit plans," "salary reduction plans," or "pretax spending accounts."

Providers should encourage parents to take advantage of these plans if they are offered by their employers. Parents may not realize that their employers offer this benefit plan. Direct parents to contact their human resources or payroll office for more information. If some parents' employers do not offer this plan, urge them to talk to their employers about establishing one. These plans are simple to set up and administer, and tens of thousands of employers—large and small—have one. Employers can get further information by contacting a benefits consultant or by asking other employers who have such a plan.

You want your clients to enroll in these plans because their tax savings can filter down to you. Parents who receive a tax break can often afford to pay more for child care. Under the current rules, a parent can realize a tax savings of up to about $1,400 under this plan. In addition, if parents don't spend all the money they set aside under these plans, they will lose it. Providers should ask clients to give them any unspent money at the end of the year. You can use this money to buy equipment, open an Individual Retirement Account (IRA), or start saving for some marketing activities! See the latest edition of the *Family Child Care Record-Keeping Guide* (published by Redleaf Press) for more information and for a sample form you can use to ask for this unspent money.

As another idea, you may want to offer an incentive to clients who sign up for these plans. Offer parents a few hours of free evening care if they enroll in a plan or get their employer to offer this plan. Some employers pay the provider directly after receiving notification from the employee. Check to see if the employer offers a direct deposit plan so you can be assured of consistent payment.

Money that clients set aside in these plans cannot be carried over and applied to child care expenses in the next year. To keep good records, ask clients to sign a receipt at the end of each year summarizing the child care expenses for the year. For further details on how a provider should handle these plans with clients, see the *Family Child Care Record-Keeping Guide.*

Employees

If you have employees to help you care for children, remember that they too can spread good word of mouth about your program. Make sure your employees are aware of the positive aspects of your program and the special services you offer so they can repeat them to their friends and acquaintances. If you use a number of part-time employees throughout the year, keep on good terms with them when they are not working for you. A negative referral from someone who has worked for you can hurt your marketing efforts.

Here are some tips for encouraging current employees, past employees, and even potential employees you decided not to hire to refer others to your program:

- Give employees several copies of your business card and ask them to distribute them to potential clients.
- When you print or revise a flyer about your program, send copies to your employees and ask them to distribute some for you.
- Put the employees on the mailing list for your newsletter.
- Offer employees a finder's fee if they refer someone to your program who enrolls for several months.
- Invite employees to special celebrations (such as holiday parties, summer parties, and anniversary parties).
- Ask employees to mention your program on their Facebook pages or to "like" your program on Facebook.

When you hire employees, you can deduct their payroll taxes as a business expense. If you hire your own children under the age of eighteen, there are additional tax benefits: You do not have to pay Social Security or Medicare taxes. Your child may also not have to pay income tax on this money. See the latest edition of my *Family Child Care Tax Workbook and Organizer* for more information.

CHAPTER 5

Marketing to Former Clients

Who knows your program the best? Probably the parents and children who have been a part of your program and have moved on. Don't forget this population as a target market. You want to maintain a lasting relationship with these parents and children because they probably have positive feelings about your care. Encourage them to tell others about your program. Word of mouth is so critical because personal recommendations carry a lot of weight in the child care field. Prospective clients will listen to the advice of friends and coworkers. Remember, the measure of your success is how well children succeed in life after they leave your program. As these children grow up, use their progress as evidence that your program works. Here are some suggestions for how to promote your program through former clients and their children:

- Stay on good terms with clients when they leave. Tell them they are always welcome to return. Ask them to fill out an evaluation form. Send them a thank-you note shortly after they leave. Some parents may not like a new child care program and will want to return to yours.

- Several weeks after they leave, send clients several copies of your business card and business flyer. Encourage clients to distribute these materials to other parents. Resend business cards and flyers every year.

- Send your newsletter to parents even after they leave so they will continue to feel like they are a part of your program. Include a notice about your openings in your newsletter. Encourage parents to give your newsletter to others who might be interested.

- Offer former clients a finder's fee for referring a parent who enrolls with you. Offer cash or a gift card.

- Send a New Year's card to former clients with an update about your program in the past year.

- If you are looking for financial help to purchase new equipment (such as a swing set or computer), ask past clients for a contribution. As another option, ask former clients to donate old toys or equipment to your program. Put a list of items you need in your newsletter.

- Encourage parents to send you pictures of their children as they grow older. Ask them to write you letters describing how their children are doing. Post these photos and letters on your bulletin board, in your scrapbook, on your website, and in your newsletter (with permission).

- Send birthday cards and graduation cards to former child care children. As the children grow up, establish direct correspondence with each child. Encourage children to write to you and send pictures of themselves.

- Use former clients as references.

- Send holiday cards to former clients.

- Invite former clients to your special celebrations. This is a particularly effective way to maintain contact with them. Their participation at your celebration will have a positive influence on your current clients, and you can use the opportunity to ask them to refer other families to you.

- If you decide to offer short-term incentives for parents who enroll their children with you (a free week of child care, for example), send news about your incentive program to former parents and encourage them to tell other families.

CHAPTER 6

Low-Cost Promotions

Marketing doesn't have to cost a lot of money or take a lot of time. This chapter gives you many easy and inexpensive methods for marketing your program to potential clients, such as with flyers, signs, business cards, your website, your Facebook page, a welcome mat, and so on. (See chapter 9 for a discussion of how you can afford to pay for marketing activities.) If you decide to try a new idea, follow through. It doesn't make sense to buy 250 pencils with your business name on them if you don't pass them all out.

You may not feel comfortable using all of the ideas that follow. If you think you might feel shy about wearing a name badge with your business name, don't buy one. At the same time, don't reject an idea just because it makes you feel a little uncomfortable. Maybe no other provider in your community uses incentive coupons, which makes you feel uneasy about using them. Maybe one idea seems too exotic or too professional. Don't let this stop you. Some ideas may work for the simple reason that no one else is using them.

Business Name

Because you are a business, it makes sense to operate under a business name. Having a business name is a sign of professionalism; it communicates to your clients that you are serious about your work. Before using a business name, check your state's legal requirements for business names (usually through the Secretary of State's office). You need to register your business name only in the state where you do business. If you live near a state border and have clients from more than one state, register your business name in those states where your clients come from. In many states, if you decide to have a business name, you must register it and pay a small fee (it's tax deductible). Before allowing you to use a business name, your state may check to see that no other business is operating under the same name. If you choose to use your own full name as your business name (such as "Maria Garcia's Day Care") you may not have to register it. If you use only part of your name (such as "Maria's Day Care"), you may have to register it. Don't be afraid to use your own name as your business name. It's a sign that you are proud of who you are and what you do and that you deliver personal care for children.

You can choose a professional-sounding name ("The Small School"), a more child-friendly name ("Country Munchkins"), or a name that communicates your location ("Elm Street Family Child Care"). It's up to you. Some clients will prefer a more professional name; others will not. Some providers choose to emphasize the professional nature of their business by using words such as "learning center," "education," "teacher," and "school" in their name. It's your business, so pick a name that you like. (Note: Some states restrict the use of words like "school" or "preschool" unless you have a specific type of license. Check with your state child care licensing department.)

To give you some ideas, here is a list of family child care business names from around the country:

Aikoh's Corner

Bugg House Child Care

Building Blocks Preschool

Carney's Angels Child Care

Country Critters Child Care

Creative Learning Home Care

Day Care by Suzanne

Gramma's Critters Day Care

Harmony Child Care Services

Just Like Home Day Care

Kiddie Kingdom

Lashia's Learning Center

Li'l Britches

Little Cherubs

Log Cabin Home Child Care

Lue's Tiny Tots

Mary's Little Lambs

Mr. Mark's Day Care

Parent Reliever Child Care

Rain City Babies (based in Seattle)

Robin's Nest Family Day Care

  (the provider's name is Robin)

Safe Haven Child Care

Sandy's School Daze

Shauna's Tiny Taughts

Two-by-Two Child Care

Tykes 'n' Tots

Wee Blossom Day Care

Some providers also use a tagline below their name to help communicate the benefits of their program. A tagline is a way of communicating additional information about your business and distinguishing yourself from your competition. If you have a tagline, use it in every place you use your name, including on your newsletters, flyers, business cards, letterhead, business checks, web page, keepsakes, enrollment packets, bulletin boards, Craigslist ads, newspaper ads, T-shirts, and so on. Here are some examples of taglines:

- A home away from home
- A loving home for child care
- Where your children are always at home
- Fun for children, peace of mind for parents
- Let us maximize your child's potential
- Providing quality Christian day care
- Quality in-home child care in a licensed country setting
- Specializing in fun and learning
- The best thing to spend on children is time
- We care, we play, we learn, we grow
- We nurture the joy in every little one
- Where children explore the world at their own pace
- Where lots of love is put into quality care
- Your child's first teacher

Business Cards and Letterhead

Business cards are one of the most inexpensive ways to promote your business. Your local print shop can make them quickly and cheaply. There are several websites where you can print business cards inexpensively, including one site where they are free! Vistaprint (www.vistaprint.com) offers free business cards with specific child care designs. Other online business card resources include Overnight Prints (www .overnightprints.com), 123Print (www.123print.com), Got Print (http://gotprint .net), and Printing for Less (www.printingforless.com).

Carry business cards with you at all times and give them away to friends, neighbors, postal carriers, newspaper carriers, workers who make house repairs, and strangers you meet at parties. Give them away in grocery store lines and at the Laundromat. Give a handful of cards to your current clients so they can pass them out at work. Keep extra cards in your car's glove compartment. Give cards to everyone who is authorized to pick up children (such as friends, grandparents, and other relatives).

If you have a business name, put it on your card. The same goes for your tagline (such as "A home away from home") or logo. You may want to use clip art from software or from your print shop. List your area code along with your phone number. If you have a cell phone, pager, e-mail address, or website, put these numbers and addresses on your card as well. Some providers choose not to list their addresses for fear that someone who wants to harm children will know where to look. As another option, include only the general area you live in (such as "Crocus Hill Area") or a partial address (such as "6XX Portland Avenue") so clients will know only your neighborhood. You can give clients the exact address when they call. Be aware that some local telephone companies will give callers the address of any subscriber. You can ask to have this service blocked for your phone number. Use the back of your business card to describe your program in more detail. List some of the benefits you offer, such as education equipment, fun field trips, or special learning programs.

Some providers make magnetized versions of their business card for clients to put on refrigerator doors or file cabinets. Because of the additional expense, you may want to give such cards to clients as a courtesy only after they enroll with you. You could also buy return address labels (or a rubber stamp) with your business name on it.

Creating a simple letterhead—to use for letters to parents, follow-up notes to prospective clients who call or visit, and your contract—can help create a professional image. You can find graphics in many computer software programs or through your local print shop. Ask your clients if anyone in their family has graphic design skills they could share in exchange for child care services. Use the same colors and typefaces on your business cards and letterhead to maintain a consistent and memorable look. Consider printing your letterhead on smaller-sized paper or self-adhesive notes for your daily messages to current clients.

Business Logo

A business logo, although an uncommon marketing tool for providers, can be used to attract the attention of potential clients. A logo gives your business an additional identity that is eye-catching and fun. Your logo can be a picture of something or a graphic design of the letters in your business name. It can be taken from a drawing made by the children in your care or from clip art from computer software. (If you have a more traditional business name like Academy of Learning, don't use a child's drawing as your logo.) Some websites, such as Vistaprint (www.vistaprint.com), offer a variety of free logo designs to choose from. Your local print shop or a private consultant can design a logo for you. As another option, you can contact your local high school's art instructor, who may have a talented student who would design a logo for you for a very small fee. Your logo doesn't have to be drawn exactly to scale. The printer can reduce or enlarge your logo to fit on cards, flyers, and T-shirts. Don't use a design or picture copied from a book, magazine, the Internet, or other published resource; it is probably protected under copyright law.

Once you've designed your logo, make sure it complements the style and design of your business card and letterhead. Use your logo on all of your marketing materials, including your business flyers, T-shirts, car signs, newsletters, advertising, website, keepsakes, name badges, business checks, welcome mat, and business signs. By doing this, you will create a consistent and memorable look for your business.

Name Badge

When you are out in the community, let people know what you do. Wear a name badge when you are traveling with the children on a field trip, transporting them to school, shopping at a garage sale, attending a workshop, and so on. You can wear your badge anytime you are engaged in business activities. The most important time to wear a badge is when you are out of your home with the children in your care. If you have employees, they should also wear badges when they accompany you on field trips or other activities. People will stop you and ask about your program. Have your business card ready to distribute. Your badge should display your business name, phone number, web address, and logo (if you have one). To find the names of companies that make badges, search online for "name badges."

You also may want to have older children (preschoolers and school-age children) in your program wear name badges on field trips. For security reasons, the badges should have only your business name on them, not the child's name. Parents you meet at the swimming pool or park may be impressed to see the type of activities children in your program participate in. As added bonuses, name badges can help you spot your children in a large group more easily, and they can help raise the visibility of family child care in your community.

Business Sign

Posting a sign about your business in your front window or front yard is an inexpensive way to promote your program. The sign may attract attention from potential clients passing by on foot or in a car. Your sign should have your business name on it as well as your phone number, website address, and e-mail address. Keep your sign clean and in good repair. Repaint it when needed. Mow regularly the lawn around the base of the sign. A worn-out sign reflects badly on your business.

On some occasions, you may want to attach an extra banner to your sign—such as when you have an opening (a "Spaces available" banner), when you start offering a special service (a "Second-shift care now available" banner, for example), and when you plan a celebration (a "Welcome, neighbors" banner for a neighborhood party, for example). When a child in your care has a birthday, you could attach balloons to your sign. By adding and removing such announcements, you will attract more attention to your sign.

Before putting up your sign, however, check with your county or city government offices (or your homeowners association bylaws) to check for any ordinances or covenants that restrict business signs in residential areas. Some areas limit the size and placement of signs; others have laws that prohibit signs altogether. You should also contact your homeowners insurance agent to make sure business signs are not a violation of your policy.

For reasons of privacy and safety, some providers do not use signs in front of their home. The presence of a business sign may attract the attention of people who don't like the idea of having a child care program in the neighborhood. Sometimes unhappy neighbors will oppose your business (see pages 41–43). You should consider this possibility before calling your local government office or putting up your sign. I once helped a provider who put up a sign announcing that she had an opening in her evening care program. A neighbor complained to the county, and the provider was forced to remove her sign because it was too big and replace it with a smaller one.

You may want to put a business sign on your car window or a magnetic sign on the side of your car or van. This allows you to advertise your program while you are on the road. Driving your van full of children with a sign on the vehicle can be an effective way to reach prospective parents as you visit local parks, children's museums, and other destinations for children. You can purchase magnetic business cards and put them on the side of your car when you park at places where young parents might congregate. Hopefully, parents will take the cards and give you a call.

Again, make sure there are no restrictions in your area regarding signs on your vehicle. In addition to contacting your local government offices, contact your car insurance agent to find out about any restrictions on using your vehicle for advertising. If you live in a neighborhood that prohibits car signs, consider putting a sign up after you leave the neighborhood and then taking it down once you reach home. If you live in a neighborhood that restricts lawn signs but allows car signs, put a sign on your car and park it where it will be visible to passersby, such as in the driveway or at the curb.

You can purchase signs at a local sign shop. You can also purchase inexpensive business signs online at websites such as Vistaprint (www.vistaprint.com), Signelect (www.signelect.com), Speedy Signs USA (www.speedysignsusa.com), and 123Print (www.123print.com). You can always make your own signs using a flat piece of sheet metal or plywood and waterproof paint. Whatever type of sign you choose, make sure it looks professional.

Here are some other sign ideas:

- Put a banner on your front porch or fence.
- Write on your front window with washable paint.
- Hang a child care flag off your front porch.
- Attach a sign to your glass storm door or front door.

Business Checking Account and Checks

Although not a requirement, many providers open a separate checking account just for business purchases. When you use checks that carry your business name, people who receive them become more aware of your service. The checkout person at the grocery store, hardware store, or video store and the pizza delivery person, for example, may be potential clients. Be aware that many banks charge extra for business checking accounts.

Even if you don't have a business checking account, you should consider buying checks with a business design on them. The background design can feature a child theme or a more traditional business theme. Your bank may offer such choices. If not, you can buy your checks online from companies that sell designed checks. (To find these companies, search for "business checks" online). Sunday newspapers often contain an advertising supplement from check design companies. Some mail-order catalog companies sell checks with various designs as well.

If you have a business logo, include it on your checks. Having a business design enhances the image of your business and attracts more attention from those who receive your checks.

Business Flyer

Providers should have a business flyer or brochure to use in their marketing efforts. The flyer should introduce your program and motivate the reader to call you for further information. Most flyers will be no longer than one page, printed on both sides of an 8½" by 11" sheet. Consider using bright colors (yellow or bright lime) for the paper stock. Or you may want to purchase predesigned brochure templates that have colorful borders or designs. Use black ink for the text (never yellow, orange, or red). This will help grab parents' attention. You can design your flyer to be folded into thirds so it can be used as a mailer. Or you can design your flyer to take up half the size of an 8½" by 11" sheet. You can include two of these half-sized flyers on one sheet of paper. To reduce your mailing costs, consider printing the half-sized flyer on card stock, cutting the page in half, and sending it out as a postcard. Look at flyers from other child centers and homes to get more ideas.

Your flyer should contain the following four elements:

1   Your business name, address, phone number, and website. Some providers
prefer not to list their exact address and include just enough information so
parents know the general location of the program (see page 78). Mention
a nearby landmark so parents can quickly determine if your location is
convenient for them. Or you can say "near the corner of Grand Avenue
and Lexington Street." Parents new to your area may not know where your
specific address is, but their coworkers will probably know the intersection.
List your phone number in large type on several places throughout the flyer.
Identify the best time for clients to call you —times when the call won't be
disrupted. If you have a tagline or a business logo, include it in your flyer.

2   Three to five benefits of your program. Try to focus on benefits that say
something special about your program and that will attract attention (see
chapter 2). If you offer any special services or have special educational credentials, list them here. Don't list your rates, as they may change; you don't
want to have to regularly reprint your flyer.

3   Testimonials from parents. Using testimonials from current or past clients
can be an effective way to sell your program. Include one or two in your
flyer. You may be able to use quotations from old parent evaluations. You
can also simply ask parents to write recommendations for you. Most will be
delighted to do so. Ask permission if you want to use the parent's quotation
or name in your flyer. Make sure you get permission in writing. To protect
parents' privacy, you may want to use only a first name and last initial after a
quotation. For example, a testimonial might say, "I can't tell you how much
my daughter Geisha loved coming to your home every morning. Thank you
for everything! —Shelly M., mother of a three-year-old."

4   An attractive graphic design. You don't have to hire a professional to design
and print your flyer, but you do want it to look good. The more professional
your flyer looks, the more likely it will be picked up. (See at the end of this
section the resources for designing your flyer.) You will be handing out hundreds of copies of your flyer, and you want to make a positive impression on
as many people as possible. If you have a logo, use it prominently on your

flyer. Be cautious about using photographs; they may not reproduce well unless you print on an expensive paper stock. Drawings or other graphics usually look better than photographs. Before you use any photos of children, you must request written permission from their parents (see appendix K, "Photo, Voice, Website, Facebook, and Video Permission Form").

Your business flyer should be your primary tool for describing your program to prospective clients. Distribute your flyers everywhere. Mail copies to parents who call you for an interview. Give them to current clients and any of your employees to distribute to their friends and neighbors. There are many places to distribute flyers in your community (see page 87 for a list of community locations). Ask permission before leaving flyers at any location. If you have prepared an incentive coupon, you may want to attach the coupon to your flyer.

The following websites can help you produce your business flyer: vFlyer (www .vflyer.com), PrintMaster (www.broderbund.com/c-32-printmaster.aspx), Paper Direct (www.paperdirect.com), Flyers Easy Flyer Creator (www.flyerscreator.com). You can also use one of Microsoft Word's flyer templates or purchase Microsoft Publisher to help you create and produce high-quality newsletters, flyers, and calendars. You may also want to ask your clients if someone in their family can help you with your flyer.

Incentive Coupons

Everyone loves a sale. To attract new clients, you may want to develop a coupon that offers an introductory discount on your services. Distribute coupons as part of your business flyer, attach them to your advertisements, or pass them out like business cards. Explore the possibility of putting your incentive coupon on the back of receipts from your local grocery store. If this is too expensive, advertise jointly with several other providers and offer a coupon that is good at each program. Consider directing a coupon to a particular audience. For example, offer the coupon only to employees of a company or members of a church or synagogue near you. Make sure you put an expiration date on your coupons; they should be used as special promotions for a specific, restricted time. Don't offer coupons all the time, as this might give potential clients the wrong idea—that you are offering a discount service.

Here are some suggestions for what you could offer with your coupon:

- no registration fee
- twenty-five dollars off the first week of care
- a free evening of care

Although there are costs associated with redeeming coupons, they usually are very small compared with the benefits of enrolling additional children. Child care centers often offer incentive coupons to attract new business.

For some providers, incentive coupons are a sensitive issue. For them, the idea of an incentive coupon conflicts with the professional image they are trying to develop. These providers are more comfortable offering a free evening of care on an occasional basis, for example, as a door prize at a local charitable event. Other providers—who might be trying to fill several openings in a very competitive environment—believe that a coupon could be the deciding factor that sways parents to enroll their child.

Door Hangers

In general, parents prefer a child care program close to their home. Many potential clients probably live close to you. One advertising strategy is to distribute door hangers in your neighborhood. On the door hanger, print a brief description of your program, which can be modeled from the language in your business flyer. Print an incentive coupon on the bottom of the hanger (with an expiration date). Encourage people who don't need child care to pass on the hanger to someone who does. Use heavy paper stock and have the hanger die cut at a print shop so it can be hung from a front doorknob. Have your own children deliver the hangers after school and on weekends, or hire Boy Scouts, Girl Scouts, or neighborhood children to deliver them. If your door hangers cannot be hung from the front door, put them partway under the welcome mat. Do not put door hangers in mailboxes; it is illegal to put in a mailbox anything other than what is to be delivered by the United States Postal Service. Also check to see if there are any local ordinances in your community that prohibit the distribution of door hangers. Be aware that some neighbors may not be happy about having a child care program in their community (see pages 41–43).

Here are some websites on which you can purchase door hangers: CheapDoorHangers (www.cheapdoorhangers.com), PrintPlace (www.printplace .com/printing/door-hanger.aspx), and Door Hangers (www.door-hangers-direct .com/door-hangers.htm).

Keepsakes

Getting your business name in front of as many prospective clients as possible is a major goal of all marketing efforts. One way to do this is to distribute keepsake items that have your business name, phone number, and website address on them. (If you have a logo, include that as well.) If your keepsake is a fun or useful item, the potential client might keep it at home in plain view, where other potential clients might see it. Always be on the lookout for the latest hot item that children or parents are using; it might be a perfect keepsake.

Give keepsakes to your currently enrolled parents and past clients, as well as to current and former employees. Mail keepsakes to parents who contact you by phone or visit your home for an interview. Pass them out at Halloween, parties, picnics, and other gatherings with friends. To find companies that make keepsakes, look in the Yellow Pages or in home product catalogs, such as Miles Kimball. Many of the following keepsakes can be individualized with a child's name, which makes them perfect welcome gifts for children on their first day at your program:

aprons/smocks	Frisbees	notepads
bumper stickers	headbands	outlet covers
buttons	key chains	pens/pencils
calendars/day planners	magnets (in the shape	picture frames
can openers	of a house or your	pins
canned jam/jelly	logo)	soft-foam balls
canvas or nylon tote bags	magnetic clips for hanging	stickers
caps/visors	children's artwork on	T-shirts (for children
chip clips	the refrigerator	and parents)
coffee mugs	mouse pads	water squeeze bottles
cup holders	Mylar balloons	

At an annual NAFCC conference, a provider showed me her keepsake: a business-card-sized flip case filled with sticky-note markers. Her business name and website were printed on the cover of the case. She told me the cases cost her ninety-nine cents each.

Distribution of Marketing Materials in the Community

One of the cheapest ways for you to get the word out about your program is to distribute your business flyer in locations where parents with young children will see them. You can distribute flyers and business cards by posting them on walls and bulletin boards, leaving them in waiting rooms and lobbies, or having them published in someone else's newsletter. You may want to attach an incentive coupon to your flyer or business card to attract more attention. Flyers posted on bulletin boards get taken down regularly, so you may want to repost your flyer every few weeks. Some providers attach to their flyers tear-off slips that include their name and phone number so parents can take the reminder with them.

When you distribute your flyers, dress professionally so you will make a good impression on anyone you might meet. Someone who notices you posting a flyer may be curious and stop to talk. Be sure you have some business cards on hand to distribute. Before distributing materials, get permission from the appropriate people; some organizations have rules prohibiting the distribution of any advertisements on site. Below is a list of some of the places you might want to distribute your materials:

- apartments (for their "new resident" move-in packages)
- beauty shops and hair salons
- Boy and Girl Scout groups
- childbearing classes
- childbirth instructors
- children's doctors and dentists
- children's fairs and concerts
- children's toy stores, shoe stores, clothing stores
- churches/synagogues (where they have meetings for moms)
- colleges and universities (students, faculty, and staff)
- elementary schools (distribute flyers at kindergarten open houses, where parents often are changing providers)
- employee bulletin boards in hotels and hospitals
- employment offices
- garage/yard sales (as well as your own yard sale)
- health clubs

housecleaning services	maternity stores	Women, Infant, and
large employers (employer and employee newsletters)	midwives	Children (WIC)
	parenting classes	offices
	PTA meetings	women's organizations
Laundromats	supermarkets	YMCAs
libraries	union offices	YWCAs
local businesses	Welcome Wagon packages	

Here are some additional ways to distribute your marketing materials in your community:

- Have the postal service mail your business postcard to everyone in your area (www.usps.com).

- Pass out flyers or business cards to families attending youth sports games (ages two and up). Advertise in youth sports programs.

- Talk to your local dentists, doctors, and insurance agents about passing out your business cards or keepsakes to their clients.

- Display children's artwork in local businesses during the Week of the Young Child (in April). Attach your business name and contact information to the artwork.

- Check to see if your county has an online message board and post an advertisement (with an incentive) there.

- Find out if there is a Moms of Multiples (www.momsofmultiples.org) or Mothers of Twins (www.nomotc.org) club in your area. If so, advertise your program through these organizations. Parents of multiples often have trouble finding care, particularly infant care.

- Look in local classified ads (printed or online) for people selling baby items (such as clothes or toys) and send them a flyer.

- Look for birth announcements in your local newspaper. Use the White Pages (www.whitepages.com) to locate the family's address. Mail them a postcard.

- Tape your business card to children's books and donate them to doctor's offices, dentists, beauty salons, eye doctors, health departments, pediatrician offices, and veterinary clinics.

- Pass out flyers to your mail carrier, milk delivery person, and garbage collector.

- Ask your florist shop to put your business card in Mother's Day bouquets, or ask your pizza parlor to include one with pizza deliveries.

- During holidays, paint messages on your front window (such as "Happy July Fourth," "Merry Christmas," "Today is Flag Day," and so on).

- Put your flyer on the windshield of cars parked at Toys"R"Us, Chuck E. Cheese, and so on. Look for cars that have car seats.

- Talk to your city offices about planting flowers on city property. You may be able to put your name on a sign saying they were planted by your program.

- Find creative ways to partner with youth organizations. One provider volunteered to clean a Little League baseball field, and in return she was allowed to hang a banner with her business name outside the field during baseball season.

- Offer free child care at a local silent auction for charity.

- Talk to people in your community. One provider always made small talk with the owner of her local deli. One day the owner removed his business cards from the cardholder next to the cash register and replaced them with her business cards! Later he asked her to care for his two-year-old.

Welcome Mat

Think of all the people who come to your home: friends, neighbors, postal carriers, delivery persons, children in the neighborhood, salespersons, religious missionaries, survey takers, and so on. A welcome mat on your front doorstep with your business name, logo, and tagline on it may make some of these visitors your next clients. This is an unusual promotion idea that attracts attention. Even if some of the people who see your welcome mat are not potential clients, they may tell someone else about your business. The welcome mat even works when you're not at home. Look in home-product catalogs or on the Internet (search for "custom welcome mats") for companies that make customized welcome mats. Here are a few resources: Personalized Doormats Company (www.personalizeddoormats.com), Xpressmats (http://tinyurl.com/42vqoth), or Personalization Mall (http://tinyurl.com /3hnd9u6).

Children's T-Shirts

When you are out in your community with your child care children—such as for field trips or a walk around the block—have the children wear T-shirts with your business name on them. The children will become walking billboards for your business. In addition to your business name, the T-shirts could show your website address and logo. Use a bright color for the shirts, and add a bold design or a children's drawing to attract more attention. Don't put children's names on the T-shirts; you don't want a stranger to be able to call a child by name and draw him away from the group. Your business name, however, should be clearly visible.

Parents who see in a public place a group of happy children with colorful matching T-shirts are likely to be curious and pay attention. It is not a common sight. You'll be surprised at how often parents will stop to make a friendly comment. Use this opportunity to distribute your business cards. Wear your name badge as well.

Local Parade

Young children love parades. They offer a place where parents and children gather to have a good time. If your town has a local parade, make sure your business is in it. March in the parade with your own children, and invite the children in your care to join you.

Make sure you will be able to keep control of all the children during the entire parade; ask another adult to help you if needed. Don't be afraid to march in a parade with only one or two children; many parents will be attracted to a small program. Have the children carry balloons and wear T-shirts with your business name on them. Use a double stroller or wagon to carry the youngest children. Attach a sign with your business name and website address on the stroller or wagon. If you want to promote something special about your program, make an effort to display it. Show pictures of your large play area, computers, special events, or just pictures of happy children. Including decorations, posters, or items prepared by the children is great advertising. Visuals of what children do in your care are a clear demonstration of the benefits of your program. Bring along business flyers and business cards to distribute to interested parents you meet. Distribute keepsakes along the way.

Alumni Magazine

Have you ever sent a note to your alumni magazine telling them that you are a family child care provider? If you live close to the college, university, or other educational institution you graduated from, you should consider doing so. The best time to send a notice to an alumni magazine is when you have something special to celebrate:

- your fifth, tenth, or fifteenth anniversary as a provider
- your excitement about caring for children of other alumni
- your marriage

Include a photograph of yourself with the children. Sometimes just sending the photograph with a brief description is enough. You could also send a class note to your spouse's alumni magazine if he or she works in your business.

Paid Advertising

So far, the ideas in this chapter have been relatively inexpensive to implement. Because you only need a small number of clients to fill your program, spending a lot of money trying to reach tens of thousands of potential clients isn't wise. Advertising jointly with other providers—primarily through your family child care association—might be a good option. The cost of advertising can be shared by many providers, making it a much more practical option.

Newspaper Advertising

When most providers think of advertising, they often think of newspaper advertising. Not every provider can afford to advertise in local newspapers very often, but it may be an appropriate strategy if you are just starting out or have a sudden drop in enrollment. With the rise of the Internet, there has been a marked drop in classified ads in printed newspapers. Most classified ads have moved online (see chapter 7). That said, some local newspapers still feature active classified ad sections. In some cases, they include these ads on their newspaper's website instead of in—or in addition to—the printed edition. When considering advertising in a newspaper, look at the newspaper's print and online classified ads. Put your ad where you see the most ads. Here are some other tips to follow when considering this type of marketing:

- Consider where you can advertise most effectively at a reasonable price. Options include metropolitan newspapers, neighborhood or community newspapers, shoppers (or advertisement-only newspapers), entertainment weeklies, parent newspapers, union newspapers, and women's newspapers.

- Look to see which newspapers already contain ads for family child care homes or child care centers. You want to place your ad where parents with young children will see it. If a newspaper does not have advertisements for other child care programs, your ad is less likely to be noticed.

- In general, it is better to advertise in local newspapers—which are often published weekly instead of daily—rather than in large metropolitan newspapers in which your ad may get lost.

- Ask several providers about their experience with newspaper ads. Other providers are a great resource for information. Not everyone will have similar experiences, but you may be able to avoid some of the mistakes made by others.

- Once you have identified several possible newspapers for your advertisement, compare their rates for classified ads and display ads. Classified ads are usually four or five lines of text about your program with no graphics or images. Display ads are usually a fourth of a page or larger, with graphics. Classified ads are generally much cheaper than display ads. Because of the expense, child care centers are more likely to run display ads than are family child care programs. Even so, you may want to consider running a one-time display ad in your neighborhood newspaper to announce your opening or a new special service. Classified ads are usually cheaper during the week and more expensive on Sundays, when more parents read the paper.

- Before writing your own classified ad, closely examine other ads from child care homes and centers. You want your ad to be noticed, so don't write the same things you see in other ads. If every provider in your area participates in the Food Program and is certified in CPR and first aid, then it's probably a waste of money to include this information in your ad. Notice the language used in other ads. The ads probably describe the benefits of the programs (such as individualized attention, computer instruction, professionally trained staff, and so on).

- Keep your classified ad concise. List your business name and tagline (if you have one). Identify the ages of the children you're looking for and any special services you offer (such as night care or Spanish language instruction). Try to stress one or two significant benefits or unique aspects of your program.

- Some newspapers occasionally run special advertisement sections or supplements accompanied by short articles on parenting. Call and find out if your newspaper has such a feature. Such supplements often come out in the early fall. You may want to set aside money (say, twenty dollars a month) so you can advertise alongside other programs in this special section. If the other programs in the supplement are centers, your family child care ad might stand out.

- After your ad appears, track how many calls you receive from parents who saw your ad. See appendix C, "Parent Call Tracking Form," for a form you can use for this purpose. You should also track the impact of your other marketing efforts (such as business flyers, networking with other providers and organizations, and finder's fees) to evaluate their effectiveness. Because the cost of classified ads can add up, you'll want to watch your expenses closely.

- After running a classified ad several times, you may want to consider other options. If you received a reasonable number of calls, perhaps you should continue running the ad. If the response was disappointing, try something new. Run the ad on a different day or in a different newspaper. Change the wording in the ad to emphasize another benefit.

- Be patient. Don't expect a single classified ad to generate enough calls to fill your program. Because parents are only looking for care for a relatively short period of time, your ad has to catch them at the right moment. Newspaper advertising is only one part of your larger marketing plan.

Sample Classified Ads

"Loving, licensed home care provider with structured activities where children have fun learning. Infant and toddler openings. Crocus Hill area. Shaunna. 655-XXXX."

"Licensed family child care home open twenty-four hours a day, Monday–Friday. Experienced staff. Music teacher on site weekly. Spanish enrichment program. School readiness emphasized. A safe, fun learning experience. Chia's Little Tykes in Roseville. 954-XXXX."

"Your child will enjoy our beautiful, large backyard with numerous toys and room to explore. Mother of two looking for preschooler to join small in-home group. Child-centered activities encourage creativity. Lots of TLC. Lynne's Playhouse: 'Learning Every Day, Loving Every Minute.' Northside. 426-XXXX."

Television, Radio, and Other Paid Advertising

Here are suggestions for taking advantage of other advertising opportunities and keeping them within your budget:

- Television advertising is generally too expensive for family child care providers. But you could encourage your family child care association to approach local television stations to see if they run public service announcements for nonprofit organizations. Your association could gain publicity for the family child care field by promoting a special event (such as a clothing drive or relief effort) or by offering a child safety tip for parents. Some television stations offer viewers the opportunity to record a brief editorial viewpoint. Again, work with your association on such a project.

- Support your local public radio or television station during pledge drives. Your business name will be read on the air. This is also an activity that your association can participate in.

- Some communities have cable access television channels where citizens can appear on locally produced programs. Check out the schedule and see if the channel has a program about parenting or children. Volunteer to be a speaker. Invite the producers to tape a show at your home. Find out if the television station can tape a special event organized by your association.

- Some local radio stations, particularly public radio stations, have programs about children and parents. Volunteer to be a guest on such a program. If it's a call-in program, don't hesitate to call and voice your opinion. Be sure to identify yourself and your business name. Be a volunteer when the public radio station holds its pledge drive so your business name will be read over the air.

- Consider running an incentive coupon in local coupon books sold by nonprofit groups as fundraisers. Or encourage your family child care association to run the ad, with the incentive coupon being valid at any member's program.

- Advertising in the Yellow Pages may be beyond the budget of most providers. Because of the decline of the printed Yellow Pages, however, the cost of a single-line ad may be manageable. Look into DexKnows (www.dexknows .com), which is the online version of the Yellow Pages. Your association could run a small ad—one promoting its referral service—in either the print or online Yellow Pages. In some communities, providers must pay extra if they use their telephone for their business. A Yellow Pages listing, however, often comes with the commercial fee, which some providers may consider worth the extra expense.

- Many communities have their own telephone business directories that carry advertising and compete with the Yellow Pages. Since most parents do not use these directories, it's probably not a good place to advertise.

Be on the lookout for other opportunities to advertise your program, such as in local publications that parents read. Large employers or local unions may publish newsletters that sell advertising space. Your community might have a special event for children where you can give away stickers or other keepsakes. Ask your current clients what they read and where they go for further ideas. There are always new opportunities to advertise.

CHAPTER 7

Internet Marketing

Parents of young children today use the Internet for almost everything: to contact friends, buy things, follow the news, listen to music, and so on. Parents also use the Internet to look for child care providers! If a parent searches the web for a child care provider in your neighborhood, will she find a listing for your program? Are you on Facebook and Craigslist? Do you have a website or post online classified ads? If not, you are less likely to be found by prospective parents.

In this chapter, we will discuss how to use the Internet to promote your program. If you are under the age of twenty-five, much of this chapter will be obvious to you already. Many providers already use the Internet and social media sites to reach parents and fill their spaces. Providers who are older and did not grow up with the Internet may find the idea of using social media somewhat unfamiliar and even scary. But no matter who you are, successfully marketing your family child care business today and in the future will involve some form of social media. More and more, parents rely on the Internet to help them find an appropriate caregiver for their child. If you ignore the Internet and the various tools it provides, you will be at a disadvantage compared with your competitors. This chapter will help you overcome any fears you might have and give you key pointers on how to effectively use Facebook, Craigslist, online classified ads, websites, child care forums, YouTube, Google, Bing, and more.

"Social media" refers to the use of the Internet to communicate with others. In the context of marketing, think of social media as tools for communicating the benefits of your program to prospective, current, and past clients. I urge you to spend some time getting comfortable with the various tools described in this chapter. You don't have to use them all, and you don't have to implement these ideas immediately. If you are confused about using computers or navigating the web, seek help from another provider, a friend, or—better yet—your own children.

Updates to Internet Resources

One of the advantages of the Internet is that it delivers information quickly at little or no cost. A disadvantage is that information can quickly become outdated. By the time you read this book, for example, some of the information (such as links to website resources) may be outdated. To help cope with this problem, I will regularly post updates to the Internet resources mentioned in this book on my blog, www.tomcopelandblog.com. Check out my blog for new links, changes in rules for users of Facebook or Craigslist, and new ideas about using social media.

Facebook

Facebook (www.facebook.com) is the world's largest social networking website, with over 800 million active users. People use Facebook to communicate with friends and relatives by sharing photos, recent activities, and news about themselves. In your personal life, you may visit Facebook every day, or you may think it is a waste of time. Regardless, you should consider the variety of ways you can use Facebook to market your business. It's free! Many family child care providers have their own personal Facebook page. Some providers have a Facebook page only for their business. Some providers have both—a personal Facebook page and a separate business Facebook page. I suggest you set up separate business and personal pages. Make sure the privacy settings for your personal page are set to a high level of security.

Note: The discussion that follows is based on how Facebook worked when this book was written. For information on changes to Facebook, visit my blog at www.tomcopelandblog.com.

Using Your Business Facebook Page

Your business Facebook page is a tool to help you spread the word about your program. Parents looking for child care who know your name may look to see if you have a Facebook page. Your current Facebook friends visit your business page. Identify yourself as a family child care provider in the Facebook profile for your business. Do the same in the section titled "About Me." List whatever openings you have now or will have in the future. Include your website and e-mail address in the section titled "Contact Information." If you don't clearly identify yourself as a provider in your profile, you are missing out on a great opportunity to promote your program.

Facebook allows you to post pictures, so consider sharing photographs of your program. Show photographs of areas where the children spend most of their time. Show pictures of meals, outdoor play areas, field trips, learning activities, special events, and so on. If you plan to post pictures of children in your program, make sure you have written permission from their parents before doing so. See appendix K, "Photo, Voice, Website, Facebook, and Video Permission Form."

You can use Facebook in creative ways to promote your program. Some providers update their Facebook status daily to inform current families about what is happening in their program. They might post notes about children's activities, arts and crafts projects, meals, new equipment, and so on. Other providers post links to website articles about parenting or to other helpful resources on the Internet. Describing daily learning activities with a photo or a short note is a good way to educate parents about the benefits of your program. Type "child care" or "day care" into the Facebook search bar to view examples of provider business pages. Look at the Facebook pages of local child care centers as well for even more ideas on how to communicate with prospective and current clients.

Privacy/Confidentiality Issues

Facebook is a wonderful communications tool, but it can be misused and create problems for you. Be careful not to post pictures or comments that will offend parents and other visitors. Don't make negative comments about parents or other child care providers. If other members of your family have Facebook pages, you may want them to keep certain information or pictures private for their selected friends. You can limit who has access to your profile, pictures, and comments by using the various privacy settings. Use common sense before sharing anything on Facebook.

Posting pictures on Facebook is ubiquitous. Once photos are shared with the public on the Internet, they can remain there for anyone to see forever. Therefore, it's important to think ahead before sharing photos of yourself, your family, and, in particular, the children in your care. Getting written permission from parents to post photos of their children on Facebook is essential. In addition, don't post children's names or any other information that could be used to identify them in photographs. If you want to include a caption with your photographs, write something like, "I have a child who is biting other children, and I need help in handling this. Any ideas?" rather than, "Jerry is biting other children." Facebook allows users to "tag" photographs with people's names. Since you don't want children's names to be revealed, ask parents not to tag your photos on Facebook. Check your Facebook page regularly and remove or edit any tags that are inappropriate.

Here are other ways you can use Facebook:

- Add "Find us on Facebook" to your e-mail signature, website, flyers, and business cards.

- Ask current clients to mention you on their Facebook page to help spread the word about your program. Ask parents to "like" your business page.

- Create a Facebook group for the current families in your program. By doing so, you can send out photos, announcements, news, and other information to keep them informed. You can also create a group for past clients or clients on your waiting list.

- Send friend requests to other family child care providers, and see what they do to attract new families and share benefits with their current clients.

Facebook is a great tool for reaching new families.

Craigslist

Craigslist (www.craigslist.org) is a website that lists free classified advertisements on everything from jobs to housing to services of all kinds. Craigslist ads are listed by city and can be found in most medium to large cities across the country. More than fifty million new classified ads are posted each month, and more than fifty-five million people in the United States use Craigslist each day. Many family child care providers regularly fill their openings by advertising on Craigslist.

Child care programs are listed in the "Community" section of Craigslist. You can post a lengthy ad about your program and include pictures, which allows you to spell out the benefits of your program in some detail. For ideas on what to write in your ad, see what information other providers include in their ads. You can post a free ad on Craigslist daily, but I don't recommend doing so. Most providers should post several times a week at most. When you repost your ad, it will move to the top of the page. After reposting your ad, make sure you delete your older ad.

VFlyer (www.vflyer.com) is a company that enables you to create standardized, professional-looking classified ads that will make your Craigslist ad stand out. If you plan to include photographs of the children in your ad, be sure to get written permission from the children's parents first.

Sometimes parents will post on Craigslist that they are looking for a child care program; you may be able to fill your spaces by responding to their ads. If the parent is not a good fit for your program, you may want to ask him to tell other parents he knows about your program. This may be the time to offer a finder's fee to the parent advertising on Craigslist.

Some providers are reluctant to use Craigslist because of privacy and safety concerns. The website includes information about how to avoid scams and fraud (www.craigslist.org/about/safety). In addition, here are some tips about privacy and safety:

- When posting an ad about your program, don't list your street address, phone number, or e-mail address. You can create a Craigslist e-mail account. If the parent wants to respond to your ad, she will send an e-mail to

Craigslist, which will be forwarded to you. You are then free to contact the parent if you want.

- Instead of your address, identify your program geographically ("West Side," "Falcon Heights neighborhood," and so on).

- Include your website address so parents can get additional information.

- If you invite a parent to visit your home, don't be home alone, and don't schedule the visit during hours when you have children in your care. Conduct the first interview in the evening or on weekends when you have another adult with you.

- Ask the parent for the name and contact information of his previous caregiver.

- Learn about the experiences of other providers who have used Craigslist to promote their program.

Craigslist is a popular site for child care advertisements, and it is a place that parents use frequently to find child care. It's worth exploring.

Other Online Classified Advertising

Twenty years ago, many people bought and sold services through their local newspaper's classified ad section. This is no longer the case. Classified ads have virtually disappeared from newspapers and now can be found on the Internet. Some newspapers have their own online classified ads, but unless your local newspaper has a lot of classified ads about child care, avoid advertising there. (See page 92 for more information about newspaper advertising.)

Instead of newspapers, look to online sites that specialize in child care. Here are the most popular of such sites:

- Daycare.com: www.daycare.com

- The Day Care Resource Connection: www.daycareresource.com

- Daycare Match: www.daycarematch.com

The cost to advertise is usually free or inexpensive. Some additional sites include the following:

- Own a Daycare: www.ownadaycare.com
- Child Care Smiles: www.childcaresmiles.com
- Care: www.care.com
- National Child Care Connection: www.nationalchildcareconnection.com

Finally, a directory of child care websites on which you can post ads for free can be found at the Family Day Care Marketing website (www.familydaycaremarketing.com).

Another way to identify where to place a classified ad is to think about how parents might find a child care program in your town. You want to advertise on websites that parents are likely to visit in their search for child care. Parents will often start by going to Google (www.google.com) and typing, "Parent looking for child care in (name of your town)." Using these search terms, parents will find websites and advertisements for individual child care centers and family child care businesses, as well as listings for services such as child care resource and referral (CCR&R) agencies, nanny agencies, and other websites that offer listings of child care programs. You want your business to be included on websites that provide child care listings:

- Care: www.care.com
- Yelp: www.yelp.com
- Superpages: www.superpages.com/yellowpages
- Yahoo: www.yahoo.com
- USCity: www.uscity.net

Many of these sites offer free classified ad listings. You may be surprised to see your program already posted on some of them. These sites sometimes get lists of licensed child care programs from the state child care agency and include them on their website. Usually, you can pay a small fee to have your program more prominently displayed.

There are some non-child-care websites where you can post classified ads for your business for free or at a very low cost:

- Welcome Wagon: www.welcomewagon.com
- Merchant Circle: www.merchantcircle.com/corporate
- Manta: www.manta.com
- Ebay Classifieds: www.ebayclassifieds.com
- Penny Saver USA: www.pennysaverusa.com

The websites above are by no means a complete list of places where you can post online classified ads. Use Google to identify other websites that list child care programs. Online classified ads (starting with Craigslist) are probably the least expensive way you can expose your program to a wide audience.

Your Own Website

Increasingly, parents expect their child care provider to have a website, and this expectation will certainly continue to increase as time goes on. Most child care centers already have their own websites, and more and more family child care providers are creating their own. Establishing a website is a good way to attract and educate parents about your program. Even though parents may not find out about you through your website, many will look to see if you have a website once they hear about you. Not having a website could be the deciding factor in whether a parent chooses your program. You want to have a place on the Internet where you can introduce your business, and the best way to do this is to have a business website.

Your website is an opportunity to share more information with parents about the benefits of your program. You can describe your program's philosophy, list a typical daily schedule, show children's activities, post testimonials from satisfied parents, and explain what children are learning. Many providers show pictures of the rooms in their home where children spend most of their time. Your pictures can also highlight your outdoor play area and children's equipment. If you post pictures of any children in your care, be sure you have written permission from their parents. (See appendix K, "Photo, Voice, Website, Facebook, and Video Permission Form.") You can also use your website to communicate with current and past clients. For example, you can post your newsletter and any new policies and announcements on your website. You can also scan photos of the children and their artwork for parents to download or pass on to relatives.

Setting up your own business website is easier than you might think. If you want to own your own website, there are three basic steps to follow:

1   Get a domain name for your website. You can register your own domain name through www.domain.com. The cost is very small.

2   Choose a company to host your website and sign up.

3   Design your website.

For more information on all three steps, see the article "How to Start/Create Your Own Website: The Beginner's A–Z Guide" by Christopher Heng (www .thesitewizard.com/gettingstarted/startwebsite.shtml). Here are some examples of provider-owned websites:

- Treasures of the Heart Child Care: www.treasureschildcare.com

- Child Care by Tori: www.childcarebytori.com

- Little Acorn Child Care: www.littleacornchildcare.net

- Doodle Bugs Daycare: www.doodlebugs.tk

If you don't want to do all of the work of creating a website on your own, you can use an online service that does most of the work for you These services own your website address (domain name) and will limit what you can do with your website. If you don't want to spend time creating your own website and you want to keep things simple, however, this may be your best option. Weebly (www.weebly .com) and Wix (www.wix.com) are companies that offer free website templates. Or you can use Internet Based Family's website builder (www.internetbasedfamily.com) for a fee.

Visit the following family child care websites for ideas on what to include in your website:

- Earth's Angels Child Care: www.earthsangelschildcare.com

- Lil' Ranch Hands Daycare: www.lilranchhands.com

- Early Beginnings: www.earlybeginningschildcare.com

- Toddler University: www.toddleruniversityhomedaycare.com
- Ms. Cheryl's Classroom: www.cherylmcfamilychildcare.kids .homepagenow.com
- Tiny Tykes Playcare: www.tinytykesplaycare.com

In addition to these, search for websites of other family child care providers (and child care centers) in your area for ideas about what to include on your website. Talk to your provider friends, search the web for the names of child care centers, and ask your local or state family child care association for names of providers who have websites.

Once you have established your own website, make sure everyone knows about it. Start by informing your local CCR&R agency so the staff can add this information to your referral listing. Put your web address on all of your business advertising (such as your business cards, flyers, keepsakes, newsletters, letterhead, and business signs). Add your website's address to your e-mail signature so everyone who gets an e-mail from you will see it.

Should you share your rates on your website? Some providers do and some don't. It's your decision. As one provider told me, "I would rather have clients know my rates up front and decide whether they can afford it than have to go through the hassle of cleaning, printing stuff out, and taking time out for the interview when they couldn't afford me anyway." Providers who don't post their rates want parents to make their decision based on the benefits they have to offer, not on price.

Blogs

Some providers have created blogs to help promote their program. What is a blog? A blog is a type of website where you can post articles, stories, photos, and other information. Think of it more as an informal online newsletter where you can write about whatever you want. There are several companies that host blogs and have created templates you can use for free:

- Word Press: www.wordpress.com
- Blogger: www.blogger.com
- Blog Spot: www.blogspot.com

Here are some examples of provider blogs that you might want to check out for ideas:

- Child Care Business Owner: www.childcarebusinessowner.com
- Everyday on Purpose: www.everydayonpurpose.blogspot.com
- The Childcare Blog: www.thechildcareblog.com
- Networked Blogs: www.networkedblogs.com/topic/childcare (This is a listing of fifty child care blogs.)

You can also include a blog as part of your program's website, or you can simply add a link to your blog on your website.

Family child care websites and blogs are quickly growing in popularity as places where providers market their program. I strongly recommend you start your own.

Family Child Care Forums

An online forum, or message board, is a webpage on which people discuss topics by posting messages. Forums differ from chat rooms because the message threads are archived for later reading. There are a number of family child care forums where providers ask questions about all aspects of their business (such as, "Should I charge for holidays?" or "What do you do about a child who won't sleep?" or "Is it normal for a child to . . . ?" and so on). You can find a wealth of information and advice posted on these forums. Providers tend to be very generous and helpful in answering posted questions. You should be careful, however, about accepting advice from anyone online about child guidance and child-development issues, because they may not reflect best practices in the field as recognized by child care experts.

Family child care forums can be a useful source of marketing ideas for your business, as many of them contain regular discussion threads about marketing. New providers sometimes post questions about how they can start attracting new clients, and experienced providers sometimes ask about particular marketing strategies. It's always helpful to hear about what promotions work and don't work for other providers. You can pick out the ideas you think might work for you.

You will find popular family child care forums at these websites:

- Daycare.com: www.daycare.com (This is the most popular forum.)

- Child Care Lounge: www.childcarelounge.com

- The Activity Idea Place: www.123child.com

- iVillage Message Boards: http://tinyurl.com/78krc5d

- Café Mom's Home Daycare Provider Group: www.cafemom.com /group/1994

- My Child Fun: http://www.mychildfun.com

YouTube

In the increasingly competitive field of child care, some family child care programs are using videos to promote their program. YouTube (www.youtube.com) is the largest video-sharing community on the Internet. It's a place where you can upload videos about your program for free. You can then refer parents (prospective or current) to your videos and offer ongoing education to parents about your benefits, as a way to market your program.

Only a few family child care providers currently use YouTube to promote their program. More child care centers use YouTube than do family child care programs— but not a lot more. Here are some very short but effective YouTube ads from providers. Notice how different providers have chosen different ways to promote their program:

- Starrs Family Daycare in Apple Valley, California: www.youtube.com /watch?v=4tXWXsbYeIc&feature=related

- Pooh's Pals Home Daycare in Rancho Penasquitos, California: www.youtube .com/watch?v=PL2TTDvOFuA

- Scott Family Childcare Learning Center in Long Beach, California: www .youtube.com/watch?v=ufwYFb53sJQ

- Kathy Yasi in Seattle, Washington: www.youtube.com/watch?v=o3qYr0tMf3s

- Titis House in Winter Springs, Florida: www.youtube.com /watch?v=0VUwS0V1Ld8

To find more videos, search for "family child care homes" on YouTube.

If you post a video on YouTube, tell people about it through your website, newsletter, blog, and flyers. As in other situations where images of children are released to the public, you must get written permission from parents before posting YouTube videos with their children in them. You should also consider your own privacy and safety whenever posting videos of the inside or outside of your home. Videos may attract predators or others who may be looking for women who are home alone during the day. Do not show the street address of your home or any room that is not used primarily for child care (rooms other than your playroom, bedrooms, kitchen, and outside play area).

The Yellow Pages offers a service to help you create a business video. Visit http://adsolutions.att.com/advertising/video-profile-ads for more information. Although videos are not widely used by family child care providers today, their popularity will likely grow as parents become more sophisticated in their search for child care.

Google Places

Google (www.google.com) is the most popular search engine on the Internet. It's where people go when they want to find something. Google Places (www.google.com/places) is a free service that allows you to post information about your business that can make it easier for prospective parents to find you. It's like having a glorified business card on the Internet. You can list your address, phone number, e-mail address, and website address, accompanied by a map showing where your business is located. Because of privacy and safety concerns, many providers may be uncomfortable having all of this information freely available to everyone. If so, you can limit how much information you want to share.

Family Child Care Associations and Social Media

Whether or not you actively use some of the social media tools described in this chapter, you may want to turn to your local or state family child care association for help. These organizations can be a source of marketing assistance through their use of social media. Your association may have its own Facebook group, or it may have posted a YouTube video. The association may also have purchased online classified ads identifying itself as a source of referrals for its members. Your association may have its own website and carry member ads. The association can promote its website to parents as a source of information about children's activities and events, parenting tips, and referrals to providers.

Other Online Tools

In addition to the tools mentioned earlier, there are a number of other online tools that you can use to market your business.

E-mail

You can use e-mail in a number of ways to market your business and communicate with parents:

- Forward articles about parenting found on the Internet.
- Send pictures of the children.
- Discuss children's recent learning activities.
- Send announcements and changes in your policies.

You can send the same e-mail to all parents by creating a group list. Send e-mails with blind copies (bcc) so you don't reveal parents' e-mail addresses to each other. In the signature line of your e-mail, include your current and future openings, your web address, and other information, such as a "Find us on Facebook" link.

Other Helpful Resources

The Internet is an almost unlimited source of information on every topic imaginable, including child care marketing. I've chosen just a few sites to share with you, but you can find more with a simple search.

Online Class on Family Child Care Marketing

There are a number of online classes available on various family child care topics. I've written a self-directed online class on family child care marketing for the North

Dakota Child Care Resource and Referral Network. It is a free course, and you can find it at www.ndchildcare.org.

Website on Family Child Care Marketing

The Family Day Care Marketing website (http://familydaycaremarketing.com) is totally devoted to family child care marketing. You can also sign up to receive a list of marketing tips for free.

Google Alert

Use this free service (www.google.com/alerts) to track how your name and business name are being used on the Internet. You can get a weekly e-mail that lists Internet articles that mention your name and your business. This can be a helpful resource if others are writing negative (or positive) things about you. This service does not necessarily capture every mention of your name.

Julie Wassom's Website

Julie Wassom is an expert on marketing for child care centers, but her website (www .juliewassom.com) and free newsletter have tips and ideas that family child care providers can use as well.

Photograph Display Sites

There are free services that allow you to post photographs on the Internet and share them with families. You can set up privacy screenings so only selected individuals can see specific photo albums. These companies include Shutterfly (www.shutterfly .com) and Kodak Gallery (www.kodakgallery.com).

Daycare Hotline

This website contains a series of articles on child care marketing: www.daycarehotline .com/blog.

Safety Tips

You can find additional tips and information about keeping safe online at Get Safe Online (www.getsafeonline.org) and Wired Safety (www.wiredsafety.org).

In Conclusion

There's much more to learn about online marketing and social media than I've covered in this chapter. Because of the ever-changing world of the Internet, I encourage you to surf the web to look for the latest ideas and tips about marketing your business. Or you can keep up to date by following my blog (www.tomcopeland blog.com) and reading the regular articles I write on marketing.

I haven't discussed all of the social media tools available to family child care providers at this time (such as Twitter), but I'm sure there will be new tools in the future. The prevalence of social media use and online advertising by family child care providers will continue to grow. Don't be afraid to jump in!

CHAPTER 8

How Other Organizations Can Help

Because providers are often isolated in their own homes, they need to take advantage of every opportunity to network with organizations and individuals who can help them market their business. By working with the organizations identified in this chapter, you can find out what families want, what services other providers are offering, what age groups and neighborhoods need more services, and what marketing ideas are working (and not working). In part, this chapter is about how you can do market research to find out about your customers. Usually it costs nothing to contact these organizations and start asking questions. Without having much money to spend on advertising, family child care providers need to spend their time talking to others and asking for help in spreading the word about their program. The most important, and often most underused, organization to work with is your local child care resource and referral (CCR&R) agency.

Child Care Resource and Referral Agencies

A primary source of free advertising for your business is your local CCR&R agency. CCR&R agencies usually maintain and update lists of all regulated child care homes, centers, nursery schools, and other child care programs in the community. CCR&R counselors send out the names of child care programs to parents who call them. Your CCR&R agency may be housed in a private nonprofit organization or a government office. To find the name of and phone number for the agency in your area, contact the National Association of Child Care Resource and Referral Agencies

(NACCRRA) at 703-341-4100 or visit their website at www.naccrra.org. See appendix M for more information.

A primary mission of a CCR&R agency is to help parents find child care. If there is not enough child care available, the agency may try to recruit new providers to meet the demand. In effect, the agency may help to create new competition for your business at times. A CCR&R agency is not a placement service for child care providers; its job is not to fill your empty spaces. Some providers think that all they need to do is get on the CCR&R list and then wait for the parent calls to come. This is a mistake. Managing your enrollment is the key to your business success, and this task is solely yours. That said, your local CCR&R agency can be a tremendous marketing resource for your business if you know how to use it. Here are some ways that you can work with your CCR&R agency:

- Make sure you are listed on your agency's referral service as soon as you start your business. You may have to meet certain local regulation requirements before your name can be added to the list.

- Your CCR&R agency will collect information about your program (such as your hours of operation and the ages of children you serve) in order to match your program with parent callers. Make sure your information is current by contacting the agency at least twice a year. Sometimes data about your program can be inadvertently changed.

- If your situation changes (for example, your hours have changed, you now have a pet, you now have a toddler opening, or you just received your CDA credential), call your CCR&R agency immediately to update your file. Don't wait for the agency to call you.

- Parents sometimes search for care months before they need it. You may want to contact your CCR&R agency about future vacancies. For example, if you know you will have an opening four months ahead, tell the agency about it so they can refer your name to parents looking for care in advance.

- Take some time to talk on the phone with a CCR&R counselor at least every six months. Your local family child care association or network group might want to invite a CCR&R representative to attend your meeting to answer questions. You can learn valuable marketing information from counselors who talk every day with parents looking for child care. Here are questions you might ask your referral counselor, the answers to which can help you market your business:

— What type of care is in high demand in my neighborhood (for example, part-time care, infant care, special needs care)?

— Have any employers near my neighborhood started hiring people for second shifts or weekends?

— What hours of care do parents need that are now difficult to find?

— What can I change or add to my referral file that might attract more clients?

— Can you give me the names of providers in the area who always have full enrollment so I can contact them to ask why they are so successful? (If they won't give you a name, ask them to forward your name to these providers and encourage them to call you. Some referral counselors may be able to give you the name of a family child care network coordinator or a mentor to contact.)

— Are any child care centers about to close? (Contact such centers and ask if you can distribute flyers about your program to their clients.)

— What is the range of child care rates (by age group) for home providers and centers in my neighborhood?

— What other information do you have about fee policies, vacations, holidays, late fees, and registration fees? (Knowing just the average cost of care in your area is not particularly helpful. For a discussion about rates, see chapter 9.)

• Ask referral counselors what they tell parents to look for when choosing a child care provider. Parents are becoming increasingly savvy in their search for quality care. If you know what questions parents are likely to ask, you can better prepare yourself with good answers.

- Ask the referral counselor if the CCR&R agency has ever received any complaints about your business. If so, fix the problem if you haven't already done so. Next, try to determine if the complaint has affected how or whether the agency refers clients to you. If a complaint has had a negative impact, see what you can do to reduce the consequences. Clients usually make complaints to their regulatory agency, not to the CCR&R agency, so the latter may not have much information.

- Some CCR&R agencies offer special referral services for active military families. This may include respite care and odd-hour care. Often these programs offer providers special incentives, marketing assistance, and additional support services. For more information, visit www.naccrra.org /military-families.

- If you were taken off your referral agency's list for some reason (such as for a licensing lapse or probation), check to verify that your name has been placed back on the referral list once you are eligible again.

- Make sure you remember to record the name, address, and phone number of all parent callers referred to you by your CCR&R agency. Providers sometimes lose the name of a parent caller and ask their CCR&R counselor, "Who was that parent you referred to me last month?" The agency probably doesn't keep records of their referrals.

- CCR&R agencies sometimes offer training for parents and providers. Find out if you can distribute your business flyer at parent workshops or post it on a bulletin board that parents will see. If you are looking for a part-time substitute or regular helper, post a job announcement on the bulletin board or distribute a flyer at provider and parent workshops.

- If your CCR&R agency publishes a newsletter for parents or providers, ask if you can advertise your business in it. Find out if there are other ways you can promote your services through the agency.

- If you can teach workshops on a topic of interest to parents, ask your CCR&R agency if they can sponsor it.

- If your CCR&R agency has a library or other resources to help your business, ask about what marketing assistance or resources are available.

- Local media organizations often call CCR&R agencies to ask for names of providers for stories on child care. Tell your agency that you would volunteer to be interviewed the next time this happens.

- Ask your CCR&R agency how many times they have given out your name as a referral in the last six months or year. This information can be helpful. If your name has been given to a lot of parents but you haven't gotten many parent calls, ask why this is the case. You may learn some valuable tips. If you aren't being referred very often by your CCR&R agency, ask why this is the case. Be aware that your CCR&R agency will not give you the names of parents who have called looking for child care in your area. This is confidential information.

- Find out if your CCR&R agency surveys parents about why they chose particular providers or programs over others. If so, ask if you can see the survey results. The survey might ask parents about the importance of the following elements in their selection process:
    — the outside appearance of the home
    — the provider's manners on the telephone
    — the cleanliness of the inside of the home
    — the cost of the care
    — the number of other children present

  If your CCR&R agency doesn't collect this type of information, you may want to encourage them to do so. Such information can be useful to you in recognizing what's important to your potential clients.

- If you find that your local CCR&R agency is not being helpful to you—or, worse, is showing a bias against family child care providers in the way they administer their referral service—talk to the director of the program and try to negotiate an agreement that satisfies everyone. Your family child care association may want to handle this on behalf of its members.

As you can see, there are a lot of ways your CCR&R agency can help you if you ask. This agency is probably the single greatest resource for your business.

Your community may have other referral services (commercial and nonprofit) you may want to contact. Some large employers offer their own referral services. Your local or state family child care association may run a referral service (see the section on family child care associations later in this chapter). There are also a number of local and national child care referral services online (see chapter 7). Find out if any of these organizations can help you in the ways identified above.

Competitors

You are in competition with many other child care programs: regulated family child care homes, child care centers, nursery schools, Montessori programs, legal but unregulated providers, illegal providers, after-school programs, religious programs, employer-sponsored programs, and others. It is a fact of life that your business will always have competitors. But there is a good side to competition that you should take advantage of as you market your business. Here are some tips on how you can learn from your competition and even cooperate in ways that will benefit both you and your competitors:

- To keep in touch with client needs, talk regularly with local competitors about trends, new services, and other changes in the field. You may pick up some ideas that will help your business.

- Find out which programs in your neighborhood (home-based programs and centers) have waiting lists and which have openings. Let the programs with waiting lists know that you have openings, and ask if they will refer parents to you. Not all programs will want to do this, but sometimes a program knows, for example, that it will not be able to offer any additional infant care in the foreseeable future; this program may want to help out parents who are on their waiting list for infant care. Be aware that other programs' waiting lists may not be up to date or may not accurately reflect the parents who are now seeking care. Some parents may have already found care or will need care sometime in the future.

- Evaluate your competitors constantly, particularly those programs that seem to be successful. Ask yourself the following questions as you evaluate them: What are their strengths and weaknesses? What special services, equipment, and benefits do they offer that clients seem to want? Why should a client choose my program over my competitors' programs? How could I offer something that's slightly different from other programs?

- Keep track of the advertisements your competitors run in local newspapers and magazines (both printed and online versions), including ads from child care centers. Clip them or print them, and start a file for your records. Critique each ad by asking yourself: Why does this ad attract my attention? What language does the program use to describe its benefits to clients? How is my program different from or similar to this program? If you decide to run an advertisement, review your file for ideas. You will often find that your family child care program has many, if not more, of the benefits promoted by large centers that may advertise heavily (see page 21). You can use your competitors' advertising to help you figure out what to emphasize about your program.

- Identify high-quality programs in your area and arrange to visit them. Most people like talking about themselves and their business. Ask for their opinion about why they are successful. Listen for ideas you can use.

Ways to Cooperate with Competitors

Although it may seem strange at first, cooperating with your competitors can be beneficial for both of you. Here are some examples:

- If your program and a competitor's program complement each other (for example, you provide infant care but not school-age care, and they provide school-age care but not infant care), try to come up with a plan for referring clients to each other when it's practical. Just because you compete in one area doesn't mean you can't cooperate in another area.

- Cooperate with your competitors—and enhance your services—by sharing activities such as field trips, special events, and celebrations. Share transportation arrangements and use employees to spread the work so everyone can have a fun time. As an added bonus, the children will benefit from having new experiences with different children. Take turns hosting events at your programs. Use the opportunity of any unique collaborations (particularly between your program and a center) to generate media coverage. Take pictures to share with prospective clients. You can tell your potential and current clients that when they enroll in your program, their children will be able to socialize with many other children during these special activities with the local center.

• If you are willing to offer care for mildly ill children, approach a center that is close to your home with this idea. Offer to provide temporary care for sick children from the center for a fee. In exchange, ask the center to give you exclusive referrals or access to some of their services, such as a van for transportation. You may want to start offering specialized sick-care services for a number of centers and homes. Before offering any sick care, however, check with your current customers to see if they have any objections. Also check to see if your local and state child care regulations permit this.

• If you occasionally use a substitute caregiver as a backup, you may want to share the substitute with a competitor so the substitute works regularly and is available to both of you.

Family Child Care Associations

All family child care providers should join a family child care association. Most providers live in an area where there is a local association. Some states have a state family child care association. There is also a National Association for Family Child Care (see appendix M for contact information). Providers should consider joining associations at every level they can. Two of the primary goals of a family child care association should be to market family child care as a service to clients and to help providers market their individual programs. Whether the association is a large, state-wide organization or a small support group, here are some ways the association can help market family child care programs.

Association Benefits

Associations can provide a number of advantages to providers and parents that are too expensive or too impractical for individual providers to offer:

- Associations can offer referral services for parents to association members. They may run local advertisements about this referral service and have a volunteer handle the parent calls. This can be an effective way to spread the cost of advertising. Associations that collect information about provider rates as part of their referral services should be aware of the legal issue of price fixing. Competitors cannot share information with each other about rates. For further details about how rate information can be collected and used, see page 170.

- Associations can purchase bulk quantities of marketing materials such as business cards, keepsakes, and name badges to help cut costs for members.

- Associations can develop general business flyers for association members to distribute to parents. These flyers might cover topics such as the benefits of family child care or how to choose a child care program. Members could put a sticker with their name and address on these flyers and pass them out to prospective clients. These mass-produced flyers would be relatively inexpensive for each provider, and they would raise the visibility and positive image of the family child care field in the community, especially in areas where competition with centers is heavy.

- Associations can promote themselves. They produce their own flyer with a title such as "The Benefits of Joining the ABC Family Child Care Association." The larger the association is, the more it can do to help its members deal with other organizations, such as government agencies, CCR&R agencies, the media, and employers.

- Associations can publish their own printed or online newsletter. Such a newsletter can be a place where members share stories about successful or unsuccessful marketing efforts. Smaller associations may not publish a newsletter.

- Associations can establish their own website to keep their members informed about legislative changes affecting providers, other resources and services available to providers, training opportunities, and how other providers are successfully marketing their program. Use the website to network with other providers. The Minnesota Licensed Family Child Care Association (www.mlfcca.org) has a particularly comprehensive website.

- Associations can offer access to tangible services and products through outside vendors, such as insurance (homeowners, liability, vehicle, disability, and umbrella liability), tax preparation services, and financial planning services.

Association Activities

Family child care associations offer activities that may help you market your business. Here are some examples:

- Many family child care associations sponsor home tours for their member providers. Groups of providers may visit several different homes of association members on a Saturday, for example. A home tour is an opportunity for you to see how other providers present themselves and pick up tips for improving your program.

- Many child care providers are exempt from state regulations because they only care for a few children. Your association may want to encourage these exempt providers to become part of your association. Most associations currently limit their membership to regulated providers. In the long run, however, this restriction may not serve the interests of family child care. An increasing number of child care providers are caring for children in their home outside of the regulation system. Associations can reach out to these providers and offer them many services: support, training, access to resources, and more. By doing so, associations can increase their membership and gain greater recognition for their advocacy efforts. Some providers will oppose including exempt caregivers in their association because doing so could be seen as undermining the quality standards of the field. Associations may want to consider including exempt providers in a secondary role. This issue is complicated, but it is worth discussing with your local association.

- Your association can negotiate with your local CCR&R agency to add questions to parent and provider surveys. Your association could, for example, ask the CCR&R agency to collect more detailed information about provider rates and why parents choose particular providers over others. This information can help with marketing.

- Your association can tackle zoning laws and homeowners-association covenants to allow family child care in all residential areas. This is a long-term project that would require substantial lobbying efforts, but it is needed in many states. Currently, only a few states have laws that prohibit city and county governments from restricting family child care providers from running businesses out of their homes.

- Associations are the most effective group to lobby on behalf of providers. A group of providers speaking as one voice is more powerful and has more influence than individuals speaking separately. Your association can lobby the government office that administers child care subsidies for low-income clients to speed up payment delivery, or it can lobby the state to increase standards of quality for all providers.

- Your association can work with the local news media to increase public attention for family child care. Positive media coverage makes it easier for all providers to market their programs. One person in the association should be responsible for making all media contacts. Here are some examples of association activities that could attract the media:

    — Sponsor a late-summer clothing drive for back-to-school clothes for low-income children in your community. Take pictures of association members dropping off clothes at the Salvation Army or other charity. Ask a local radio station or newspaper to cosponsor this event.

— Organize a relief drive to provide assistance during an emergency (such as an earthquake, fire, flood, or hurricane). Collect toys, clothing, and food for children of needy families and distribute them through the Red Cross. These activities can help parents in your community associate concern for children with family child care providers.

— Celebrate the anniversaries of providers who have been in business fifteen, twenty, and twenty-five years. Submit photos of anniversary celebrations to local weekly or daily newspapers and radio and television stations.

— Organize a fundraising campaign during Halloween by having trick-or-treaters carry a donation can for a local charity.

At least once a year, associations should conduct a survey of their members to evaluate the association's own work. The survey should ask members what additional benefits and activities they want the association to focus on. It should ask members to prioritize current benefits and activities. The work of marketing to its members should be an ongoing activity of all associations.

In addition to family child care associations, a growing number of organizations, networks, systems, and support groups are organizing to help their members. The largest organization of child care professionals and early childhood educators is the National Association for the Education of Young Children (NAEYC). Each state has an affiliate chapter. NAEYC is not primarily focused on serving family child care providers, but some of its state and national conferences have workshops for providers. In some states, providers play a more active role. For more information, see the contact information for NAEYC in appendix M.

The largest employer-supported child care program is the US military, with family child care systems organized within each service branch. The Head Start program increasingly works with providers around the country. Monday Morning America (800-335-4MOM) is a family child care provider management service. Shared services is a newer idea—where child care centers and family child care providers work together to share costs and deliver services in a more efficient manner. For more information, contact the Alliance for Early Childhood Finance (www .earlychildhoodfinance.org) or visit their website. There may be other state or local networks or projects in your area. Joining these networks when you can is a way to access resources and support that can help in your marketing efforts.

Addressing Illegal Child Care

No child should be cared for by a person who is operating in violation of local child care laws. This is a simple goal that I think all family child care providers, parents, and organizations in the early childhood field should support. By "illegal child care" I mean care that is offered by someone in violation of state laws. (State laws vary greatly, so the definition of illegal care will vary from state to state.)

My definition of illegal child care does not include regulated child care providers who are in violation of a particular state rule (for example, overenrollment). It also does not include exempt child care, which is care that is not required to be regulated by the state (kith and kin care, relative care, and so on).

Illegal family child care is widespread, and it undermines the reputation and quality of care for the entire child care field. It also creates unfair competition for those who follow the rules. Many licensed child care providers are reluctant to address this issue. But because we all agree that children should not be cared for in an illegal setting, it is up to us to take action for the sake of these children. I believe that the family child care field should make ending the practice of illegal child care a priority. Individuals who are operating illegally should either become regulated under state law or should be shut down by local authorities.

Family child care associations, on the local, state, and national level, are in the best position to tackle this challenge. I propose a two-step plan for addressing this problem:

1   Education
2   Enforcement

Step One: Education

Family child care associations should talk with their local CCR&R agency and their local child care regulatory agency about the issue of illegal child care. Because some parents and illegal child care providers do not understand what is and is not legal, these organizations could initiate a joint community education campaign. This campaign should educate parents and child care providers about the benefits of regulated child care. It should also define the differences between illegal, exempt, and regulated care in your area. The campaign could develop flyers that explain these differences. Another idea is to insist that all classified ads in local newspapers and online referral services, such as Craigslist, post a definition of what legal child care is and forbid illegal caregivers from advertising. Family child care associations have an interest in seeing illegal caregivers comply with the law, because they can then recruit them to become association members.

Make it the job of a specific association board member or staff member to become the point person for this activity. The point person's job is to check classified ads and notices on bulletin boards, in grocery stores, and at Laundromats for illegal providers. Association members who hear about such providers can give the names to this point person. The point person can then contact this illegal provider, explain the regulations, and offer to help the provider become legal. If, after awhile, the person refuses to cooperate, the point person should report that person to a regulatory agency.

This education effort should also include a plan for how the public can report illegal child care providers and what local regulatory agencies will do in response. Approach local media outlets and seek their cooperation in publishing or broadcasting stories about your campaign. Ideally, local authorities will inform illegal child care providers that they must become regulated or they will be shut down. If a child care provider refuses to shut down, local authorities should take legal action to enforce the law. If there are problems within the regulatory system that make it difficult for providers to become legal (such as a lack of licensing staff, housing barriers, undocumented workers, and so on), work with local government officials and your CCR&R agency to try to overcome them.

Child care providers should work through their local associations to establish a cooperative partnership with their local CCR&R and child care regulatory agencies to pursue this public education campaign.

Step Two: Enforcement

If your association does not receive cooperation from local regulatory agencies—or these agencies are not willing (because of budgetary or other reasons) to take actions that shut down illegal child care programs—it should discuss what enforcement actions can be taken.

Again, providers who are exempt from state regulations are not operating illegally. Illegal child care providers are individuals who are required under state law to be regulated (or licensed) and refuse to become so. These providers are creating unfair competition to your program. More important, they are probably not offering a safe environment for children, and your regulatory agency should know about it. Local regulation departments may be understaffed and have little time to enforce the rules. If regulators in your area do not aggressively try to close down illegal providers, you may want to talk to the politicians who oversee this department. The appropriate person may be a county commissioner or a state representative. When expressing your concerns about illegal providers, stress the fact that state and local governments are probably losing tax revenue, because illegal providers are probably not reporting all of their income. In addition, illegal providers are not eligible to participate in the Child and Adult Care Food Program (CACFP), which can bring in more than $11,000 of federal money per child per year. Local governments may also be liable for injuries to children in illegal programs if they know about an illegal operation and fail to close it down. Talk with your local police department about this problem as well. After all, this kind of care is against the law!

If none of these efforts leads to effective action against illegal child care, then your association should report these illegal caregivers to the Internal Revenue Service (IRS). I have spoken with IRS officials about this issue, and they are aware that some child care providers are not reporting their income. They want to hear about illegal child care providers so they can recover unpaid taxes. Call 800-829-0433 and talk to an IRS agent, or write to the IRS to report an illegal caregiver. No matter which method you choose, the IRS will hold your name in confidence. You do not have to identify yourself when turning in an illegal caregiver.

If you write to the IRS, you can use **Form 3949A Information Referral**, which asks you to answer a few simple questions about the illegal child care provider. You do not need to know the illegal child care provider's Social Security number or have proof that the person is not reporting all her income. You may also simply write a letter to the IRS instead of filling out this form. Send your correspondence to the Internal Revenue Service, Fresno, CA 93888. Again, you do not have to identify yourself in your letter. For more information, see the IRS online article "How Do You Report Suspected Tax Fraud Activity?"

An IRS official informed me that the IRS is more likely to investigate a claim if they hear from more than one person. Therefore, I suggest that child care providers ask several members of their association to fill out **Form 3949A** to report an illegal program. If the IRS investigates the provider and discovers unreported income, it will take action to collect this income.

Child Care Regulators

Family child care regulations vary greatly from state to state. If you have a license or registration system, you probably have a government worker who is responsible for monitoring your program. You may or may not see this person on a regular basis. Here are some tips for working with your regulator:

- Make sure you keep in compliance with all child care licensing rules. Don't give clients a reason to complain about your program. Don't give your regulator a reason to speak negatively about you when prospective clients call for information about your program. Maintaining a high-quality program starts with following all government regulations and laws.

- Sometimes regulators survey parents who are using your program as part of their relicensing process. Ask your regulator to tell you what kind of feedback has been received from parents. Use any highly favorable comments about you and your program to help you identify some of your benefits. Use any negative but fair comments as an opportunity to identify ways to change your program.

- Check with your regulator to see if any clients have submitted complaints about your program. You may not otherwise be aware that your regulator has conducted an investigation in response to a complaint about your program. If there has been a complaint against you— even if the complaint was found to be unsubstantiated—this may be a part of your file, which is public information. Ask your regulator exactly how any negative information in your file is communicated to a prospective client. You may want a friend posing as a parent to call the regulator to ask about your record and see what the regulator says about you. Most regulators probably have a lot of leeway in how they can share negative information with callers.

- Ask your regulator for advice about how you might attract new clients to your program. Your regulator has probably seen many other programs and should be able to point out some ideas that have worked for other providers. Don't be afraid to ask direct questions, such as, "What do you think are my strongest points as a provider?" "What aspect of my program do you think I might change in order to attract more clients?" and "Do you know how other providers have been successful in attracting clients?" You may be able to use the answers to help you identify the benefits of your program.

- Ask your regulator for the names and phone numbers of several successful providers who run quality programs and have full enrollment. Call these providers and ask if you can visit them to talk about why they are doing well. Depending on local or state rules, regulators may not be allowed to give out other providers' contact information. If that is the case for you, request that your regulator pass your contact information to the providers so they can get in touch with you.

Dealing with Negative Information in Your File

Here's an example of how to deal with negative information in your file. Let's say your file shows that two complaints were made against you five years ago about a lack of proper supervision at your program. Apparently, a client who was unhappy about having to pay late fees filed a complaint on two different occasions after leaving your program. She told your regulator that you let the children play outside alone while you were preparing lunch. Your regulator investigated and found that you had not violated any rules, and no action was taken against you. So when a parent calls today asking about you, your regulator could respond in several ways:

- "We've received two complaints concerning a lack of supervision."

- "We've received two complaints concerning a lack of supervision that occurred five years ago."

- "We've received two complaints made by one person five years ago that were unsubstantiated; we took no action against the provider."

- "No substantiated complaints have ever been made against this provider. After three years, we do not keep records concerning unsubstantiated complaints."

All of the above statements are true, but it's which one the regulator uses that can make a big difference in whether the parent calls you for an interview. If you are unhappy about how your regulator responds to parent callers, discuss your concerns with the regulator and offer specific suggestions for presenting a more balanced picture of your program. In the previous example, you might ask the regulator to always mention that the complaints were unsubstantiated, they happened over five years ago, and no negative action was ever taken against you. If you are unable to reach a satisfactory solution with your regulator, talk to a supervisor. It is important for regulators to represent your record fairly. Not doing so can have a significant negative impact on your program.

Food Program Sponsors

Providers who are not already participants of the Child and Adult Care Food Program in their area should join immediately. The food reimbursements offer a significant financial benefit to your program (see the *Family Child Care Record-Keeping Guide* for details). The nutritious food that you serve as part of the Food Program promotes the health of the children in your care. The Food Program can also be used as a source of marketing support for your program:

- All Food Programs offer training workshops on nutrition, and many also offer workshops on a variety of topics that may enhance your business. Attend as many as you can. At these workshops, talk to other providers about how they market their services and ask what they are hearing about the needs of parents.

- A representative from your Food Program will visit your home at least three times a year to monitor your compliance with the program's regulations. These representatives accumulate a lot of knowledge about family child care because they visit numerous providers each month. Use this opportunity to talk with the representatives.

- Ask the representative for tips on how you might improve your business. Ask questions such as, "What do other providers do to market their program?" and "How can I make my program more attractive to clients?"

- Ask the representative for the names of other providers who offer high-quality care and have a waiting list. Visit these providers to learn more about why they are successful.

- Ask the representative if she knows other providers who offer special services: "What client needs do you think I might be able to fulfill?"

- Ask the representative if she senses any trends in the child care field: "What have you heard about new child care programs opening (homes and centers), changes in hiring by local employers, or changes in governmental assistance programs for low-income clients?"

- Your representative will fill out a home-visit report, which contains information such as how good the food looked, how well the children washed their hands, and how the children behaved at the lunch table. You can use this report to market your program to parents; show parents how well you were rated by posting the report on your bulletin board and in your scrapbook.

- When marketing your program to parents, emphasize the nutritional benefits children receive because you are on the Food Program. If your Food Program offers additional services—such as tips on cooking, gardening, and using fresh food—mention how these benefit their children as well. Because a large percentage of regulated providers are on the Food Program, your participation may not distinguish you from other providers, so it has limited value as a marketing promotion. In this case, you should emphasize other benefits of your program. If you compete with a lot of unregulated providers who are not on the Food Program, however, it becomes more relevant to stress the advantages of being on the Food Program.

Government Child Care Subsidy Agencies

Most states have government subsidy programs to help poor working families pay for child care services. Such programs are usually administered by a local governmental unit (usually the county) or in some cases by a private nonprofit agency. Many parents who receive this subsidy use family child care providers. Because they work for these programs and are in regular contact with parents looking for child care, social workers or case managers can be a valuable resource for you:

- Find out if you are eligible to participate in the subsidy program in your area. Check to see if there are any special requirements you must first meet. Get a copy of the rules governing this program so you can find out when to expect payments. Find out whether you can charge clients the difference between what the county pays and what you charge other clients. If you can charge the difference, you should consider doing so. Determine if you can require clients to pay in advance, if you can receive higher payments if you care for children with special needs, and so on. Although it is a violation of the Americans with Disabilities Act for you to charge clients more to care for children with disabilities, the government can pay you more to care for such children.

- Talk to the social worker about how you might attract more clients who receive child care subsidies. Ask questions such as, "Do you hear comments from parents about what they are looking for in a child care provider?" and "What can I do to get more low-income parents to visit my program?" Expressing your interest to social workers may encourage them to give your name to the next parent who comes to their office.

- Ask the social worker if there are bulletin boards in the agency's office where you can post your flyer. Ask if the agency distributes a parent newsletter in which you can place an ad.

- Sometimes the rules governing these subsidy programs can create hardships for providers. For example, sometimes providers have to wait months before being paid, and some subsidy programs have no recourse for collecting payments from parents who leave a program without paying. Talk with a social worker about any problems the agency is experiencing. If the problem is serious enough, you may want to work through your family child care association and lobby the government unit for reform. Even though dealing with these subsidy programs can be frustrating at times, you should think twice before throwing up your hands and refusing to care for these children. Low-income parents can be a consistent source of customers for your business.

Unions

In recent years, the number of states that have unions for family child care providers has increased. These unions include the Service Employees International Union (www.seiu.org); American Federation of State, County, and Municipal Employees (www.afscme.org); and the American Federation of Teachers (www.aft.org). Consider contacting these organizations to see if there is a union presence in your state.

Unions have traditionally worked to help increase the rates paid by the state to low-income parents receiving child care assistance. In addition, they have helped to increase providers' access to training and improved licensing standards. Since union activities are directed by its members, you may want to suggest that your union offer marketing assistance by printing low-cost marketing flyers, offering discounts on keepsakes, and launching a campaign against illegal child care. Union efforts should support local and state family child care association activities as well.

Community Organizations

Compared with other businesses, you are at a disadvantage in marketing your program because you have so few clients. Child care centers, with many more clients, have an easier time generating positive word of mouth. Family child care providers, who care for only a few children at a time, may have to work harder to market their program. To help in your efforts, work with a variety of community organizations to reach prospective new clients.

Share the word about your program with organizations where prospective new clients might be found. Or connect with an employee at one of these organizations and find ways for him to spread the word about your program. See page 87 for a listing of the many locations where you can distribute your marketing materials. Below is a listing of the types of organizations and businesses you should consider approaching.

Religious Institutions

If you are a member of a religious institution, start there. Then stop by other churches, synagogues, or mosques in your neighborhood. Introduce yourself to the office assistant who welcomes new parishioners and receives calls from parishioners seeking child care. Ask if you can post a flyer on the bulletin board, put a listing in the church bulletin or newsletter, or distribute business cards at social events and community charity activities (particularly those involving children and parents). Volunteer to work in the nursery during services so parents can observe you caring for children firsthand.

Diaper Services

New babies will soon need child care services. Distribute business cards, incentive coupons, keepsakes, and business flyers through your local diaper services. Search the Internet for these services, or look in the Yellow Pages under "diaper services."

Elementary Schools

Visit your local school and talk with the office staff. Let them know you are in business, and ask if you can leave business flyers for parents and staff. If you offer sick care, mention this. Some parents will be happy to know that a child care provider lives near the school. Join and participate in local parent-teacher association (PTA) functions. Your face and name will become more familiar. Post flyers at kindergarten open houses.

Employers

Start by approaching employers of your current clients. Ask the employers if they sponsor on-site community fairs or publish employee newsletters where you could write an article on a parenting issue or place an ad. Some large employers have their own in-house referral service. Introduce yourself to the staff responsible for running the service. If you are not already on their referral list, ask what it would take for you to be on it. Ask if they would distribute an incentive coupon from you to all new employees.

Hospitals

Maternity wards are great places to distribute incentive coupons, business flyers, and keepsakes. Ask if the hospital gives out baskets of items to new parents. Many parents of young children work in hospitals, so you should find out if you can distribute information about your program on employee bulletin boards, in newsletters, or through union activities.

Moving Companies and Real Estate Offices

When a new family moves into a neighborhood, it can mean new business. Give your incentive coupons or business flyers to moving companies and real estate offices in your area and ask them to pass them out to their customers. You may want to offer a free day of child care on moving day for new parents coming into your community.

Obstetrician/Pediatrician Offices

Approach these offices near you and ask if they have any health or safety brochures you can distribute to your customers as a service. Give them your incentive coupons and business flyers and ask them to distribute them to new parents. If you have a special service for babies, highlight this in your materials.

Welcome Wagon

Organizations such as these should be happy to distribute incentive coupons and keepsakes for your business (www.welcomewagon.com).

Chamber of Commerce

Chambers of Commerce are associations of businesses, and most of their members are small businesses. Because you are a small business, it makes sense to join your local Chamber of Commerce. Here are some ways your Chamber can help you to market your program:

- Most Chambers sponsor regular "get acquainted" gatherings for new members. These gatherings offer a great opportunity to meet employers who have employees needing child care services. Bring plenty of business cards and business flyers describing your program. Since there will probably be very few other providers who are members of the Chamber, your presence will likely attract attention.

- Chambers usually offer conferences and workshops on a variety of business topics throughout the year. Although most of them may not be of particular interest, attend several to learn more about business trends in your community, meet new people, and distribute your business cards.

- Find out if the companies closest to your home are members of the Chamber. If so, make a point of introducing yourself to a company representative at some Chamber event. Your chance of being able to distribute flyers at an employer's work site are greatly increased if you establish a business relationship through a professional organization such as the Chamber.

- Find out if any advertising or marketing agencies or consultants are members of the Chamber. Approach them through Chamber events and ask them if they ever work for small businesses like yours at a discount. Perhaps these companies offer workshops that are open to the public. Some consultants may be interested in helping you or your family child care association with such projects as designing a newspaper advertisement or reviewing your business flyer.

- Some Chambers have programs in which retired executives offer their services to local businesses or nonprofit organizations for a nominal fee. The Small Business Administration (SBA) has a similar program that is free. Even if you are not eligible to receive assistance from this program, your family child care association might be. If so, ask for help with marketing-related services. The benefit of these programs often depends on the particular person involved, so screen the program before agreeing to participate.

Generating News Coverage

You may be able to get free publicity if a local news organization decides to run a story about your program. Having a television station, newspaper, or radio station cover your program may not be as far-fetched as it might seem at first. News organizations are always on the lookout for stories, and human-interest stories about children are often very appealing. But you have to have a "hook" to attract the media's interest. That is, you need to have something newsworthy or something that is interesting to view. A story on children learning about farm animals sounds boring. But a picture of young children touching a huge pig can be interesting. Years ago, a child care center in St. Paul, Minnesota, was featured on a local news program for bringing a pig to the classroom.

Here are some ideas for stories your local news organizations may want to cover:

- Your program plans to visit a nursing home to sing songs during the holidays.

- You are throwing a party to celebrate the twentieth anniversary of your first day as a provider. Invite a local politician to attend to attract more media coverage.

- You are having a "Safe Halloween" party at your home for neighborhood children and have a clown or singer to entertain them.

- You are planning to take special field trips with the children to the state fair or to local businesses.

- Your program plans to attend a local history or community celebration, such as Strawberry Days or Founder's Day.

- The children are scheduled to plant flowers at local monuments or cemeteries on Memorial Day.

- You and the children plan to pick up litter at your local school playground or park.

- You and the children will participate in a Bunny-Hop-a-Thon for the Muscular Dystrophy Association.

- You are organizing an all-green Ring-around-the-Rosie Marathon for the children on St. Patrick's Day.

You can take pictures of the children during a seasonal activity—such as building a snow fort after the first blizzard, picking apples in September, choosing pumpkins in October, and taking holiday decorations to nursing homes in December—and submit them via e-mail to the assignment desk at your local newspapers and television stations. Make sure to request written permission from parents before submitting any photographs of their children. (See appendix K, "Photo, Voice, Website, Facebook, and Video Permission Form.")

If your picture or story appears in a newspaper, make copies of it and put it in your newsletter, post it on your bulletin board, add it to your parent enrollment packet, link to it on your website and Facebook page, and paste it into your scrapbook. Make sure you put a caption with your business name on the picture or story so your business will be clearly identified if a parent passes copies to friends or relatives.

Don't get discouraged if the media don't pick up on your first ideas. Keep trying. Submit pictures or story ideas at the beginning of the month so they can be used later if space is available. Ask news professionals what kind of stories they are interested in. Just by introducing yourself, you invite a call for help when the next breaking story on child care comes around.

Handling Negative News Coverage

Occasionally the news media will write a story about a terrible incident of child abuse or child neglect in a child care home or center. Any negative story hurts all child care programs because it undermines the confidence of parents now using, or considering using, family child care providers. Whether such a negative story originates from a national or a local event, you should consider responding to it. Try to counter all negative stories with something positive, or at least explain why parents should not fear all family child care. It may be difficult for you to do much as an individual, so it is best if your local family child care association can respond to negative news coverage. Consider the following ideas for reassuring clients about any negative press:

- Keep your current clients informed about negative news coverage. Write a short note about the news story and post it on your bulletin board and in your newsletter. Don't go into detail about the child abuse or neglect. Write about why this incident would not occur in your program. Here are some ideas:
  - You are a regulated provider, and the provider in the news story is not. You can check with your local CCR&R agency to see if the provider is regulated. Remind your clients that you follow state regulations that make such incidents less likely.
  - You have a small number of children that you can easily supervise.
  - You have taken training to reduce your stress, or you have your spouse or a helper to assist you.

— The incident is less likely to happen in your state because the regulations in your state are stricter.

— You have an open-visitation policy with parents.

- Ask parents if they have any questions or concerns about a reported news incident. Try to reassure them that you are doing everything you can to protect their child.

- Refer parents to other resources that may provide further information (a local CCR&R agency or regulator).

- Write a letter to the editor of your local newspaper. Point out why the incident is an uncommon event or why it's less likely to occur in your community. Describe some of the positive aspects of family child care. Some newspapers run guest columns as commentaries on larger news stories. Call your newspaper and volunteer to write such a guest column.

Turn the Negative into a Positive

Whenever there is a negative national news story about family child care—even if there has been little local coverage—your family child care association should contact your local news organizations (television, newspaper, and radio) and suggest how the story should be covered locally. If the local television station has already run a story, call the newspaper and suggest a follow-up article. Here are some ideas for how to get news organizations to turn a negative story into something positive:

- Encourage the news organization to tell parents where they can find additional resources that can answer their questions and help them become better consumers. The most common sources of such information are the local CCR&R agency, regulatory office, and family child care association.

- Prepare a flyer on topics such as "How to Choose a Child Care Provider" or "How to Identify Signs of Child Abuse" and offer to send it out to parents for free. Approach the appropriate staff at the news organization and ask if they would like to send out the flyer. Offer to put the organization's name on the flyer as a corporate sponsor if they will pay for the printing and distribution.

- Refer the news organizations to other sources they should contact for follow-up stories. These could include child development experts, CCR&R counselors, and state child care regulators. These sources may have information about the number of child abuse cases that occur in family child care versus in parents' homes. With the rise in the number of children enrolled in child care settings, it's logical to assume that the number of child abuse cases in these settings will grow. But the percentage of such cases probably continues to be very small compared with those occurring in parents' homes.

- Tell the news organizations how your local child care regulations compare with those of the state where the incident occurred. If your regulations are stronger, point out that such incidences are less likely to happen in your area. Encourage a story about the importance of child care regulations and how well they can work. If your regulations are weaker, call for them to be improved. Ask your association to go on record as supporting efforts to change local regulations. Encourage the media to do a story on the importance of strong regulations and what your state or local government officials are doing about the problem.

- Establish a long-term, ongoing relationship with local news organizations. Offer suggestions for stories on a regular basis (see pages 137–38 for some ideas). Contact the media to cover the annual Week of the Young Child (in April each year), Worthy Wage Day (May 1), and Provider Appreciation Day (the Friday before Mother's Day). For further information about these events, see the organizations listed in appendix M.

- The media often refer to family child care programs as "centers." If this happens, call the reporter or anchor and educate them about the correct language to use. Television stations sometimes show pictures of a child care center whenever there is a story on child care. Call the station and explain the difference between a home and a center and point out that a majority of children are cared for in a home. Use these opportunities to educate reporters and suggest ideas for positive stories on family child care.

- Your association should be a reliable resource for information on child care issues. Make sure the association has one member who will make all media contacts. You want to make it as easy as possible for the media to get information quickly. If your contact cannot answer a specific question, the reporter should be referred to other individuals or organizations.

How to Handle Negative Comments about You on the Internet

No matter how good you are at caring for children, you will never be able to make every parent happy. Sometimes unhappy parents may write negative comments about you on the Internet. There are a growing number of places online where parents can review your program:

- ChildcareRatingz: www.childcareratingz.com
- Child Care in Your Area: www.childcarein.com
- About.com Child Care: www.childcare.about.com/od/childcarereviews /ReaderSubmitted_Reviews_of_Child_Care.htm

Look at these sites to see a variety of positive and negative reviews. There are also more general websites that offer reviews of family child care providers:

- Google Places: www.google.com/places
- SuperPages (Yellow Pages): www.superpages.com
- Yelp: www.yelp.com

What should you do when you see a negative review or comment about your program online? Here are some suggestions:

- To reduce the chance that a parent will write a negative review, do what you can to satisfy the parents currently enrolled in your program. Show gratitude for parents who stay with you. Conduct annual written evaluations or face-to-face discussions with parents and ask if there are any major problems. The sooner you identify a problem, the easier it will be to fix it.

- Try to end all parent relationships on a positive note. Inevitably, you will sometimes have conflicts when a parent leaves your program. Often this conflict is over money; for example, you might want the money that is owed you, and this makes the parent unhappy. Taking a parent to court over a few hundred dollars may not be the best move, because the parent will likely become even more unhappy, regardless of the outcome. If the parent seems particularly upset or vindictive, do whatever you can to address the parent's concerns and not sue him. If there is nothing reasonable you can do to satisfy the parent, don't say or do anything that will aggravate him further. The only sure way to avoid most money conflicts is to require parents to pay for the last two weeks of care in advance.

- Contact your licensor if a dissatisfied parent is leaving your program. This can help reduce the impact if a parent complains to the licensing office later.

- Ask parents to write positive reviews about your program on your Facebook page and the various child care review websites listed earlier.

- Ask parents to give you written recommendations and request permission to post them on your website or blog.

- When you receive a negative review, ask the parents in your program to post positive reviews on the same website.

- If a negative review states information that is untrue (for example, you are accused of breaking your contract when you clearly did not), you can ask the website's host to take down the review. Not all sites will do this. If the reviewer invades your privacy (by listing the name of your own child, for example), you may have a better chance of getting the negative post removed.

- If a negative review contains only minor criticism, don't directly respond. Let the parents in your program respond for you. If the criticism is severe, untrue, or unfair, reply directly on the same website. Don't be confrontational or aggressive in your response. Don't say that the parent is lying or use hostile language. Instead, post something like this:

— "I'm sorry you were unhappy with my services."

— "I think we had a difference of opinion about how to respond to your child's behavior. I hope you find another caregiver who meets your needs."

— "Your description of my actions toward your child is inaccurate. I have contacted my licensor about your accusations, and she has not taken any action against me. You may want to contact her about this." (If the parent doesn't contact your licensor, you can write another comment several weeks later: "My licensor has informed me that you have not contacted her in the last two weeks about the care your child received from me.")

- If the criticism of you is defamatory (that is, damaging to your reputation or a statement of untrue information, not opinions), you may want to consult a lawyer. In general, you should avoid starting a lawsuit, but a lawyer can advise you of your legal rights. See the *Family Child Care Legal and Insurance Guide* for information on how to find and use a lawyer.

At the time of this book's publication, online reviews of family child care providers are somewhat rare. I expect online reviewing to grow more popular with parents in the years ahead. Remember that most minor criticism can be ignored. Try not to take negative comments personally. You can't make everyone happy. Let the parents in your program respond with positive comments.

CHAPTER 9

How to
Set Your Rates

In a national survey, parents using family child care were asked, "If your provider asked for five dollars more a week, would you be able and willing to pay that additional amount, or would you look for another provider?" If parents said they would pay the extra five dollars a week, the survey automatically asked the question again, raising the proposed amount by another five dollars a week. The survey continued to ask the question, increasing the amount each time, until the parents finally said they would look for another provider. The results were surprising: 71 percent of the parents surveyed said they would pay ten to fifty more dollars per week to their current provider (see *The Study of Children in Family Child Care and Relative Care*, cited in appendix M). Does this mean that all providers should raise their rates by this amount? No. It's not that simple.

I have trained tens of thousands of providers across the country on a variety of business issues. I often ask the audience, "How many of you have lost a client because you raised your rates?" A few hands always go up. Then I ask, "How many of you with your hands raised wish you had those clients back in your program?" Virtually every hand goes down. The biggest fear providers have about setting and raising their rates is that they will lose clients to another provider. But, in fact, when this does happen, most providers do not regret their decision.

You will never see a workshop for parents titled "How to Pay More for the Child Care You Now Receive." The responsibility for setting and raising rates will always rest with the provider. For many providers this is a difficult subject, but it is an important one. Ultimately, your marketing efforts may bring children to your program, but if you aren't charging enough to meet your own needs, you may not be in business very long.

How to Think about Rates

Thirty years ago, most family child care providers charged by the hour, charged the same rate for all ages of children, did not charge parents if their child was sick, and did not charge for any vacations or holidays. Today more and more providers charge by the week, charge higher fees for infants than preschoolers, and charge for absences and some paid vacations and holidays. These trends are more pronounced in centers than in homes and are more common in urban than in rural areas. The main reasons for this change are a sharp increase in parent demand for child care and a growth in the number of providers who see their work as a professional career.

Despite these changes, family child care programs generally charge less—and in some cases significantly less—than child care centers. This difference cannot be explained by the quality of care. Many homes offer higher quality of care for children, especially for infants. The difference cannot be explained by the geographic location of child care programs or by the income level of the clients served. Homes and centers exist side by side in all communities, and both serve all income levels. The difference in rates has to do with providers' reluctance to treat themselves as a business and the failure of providers to communicate the benefits of their program to parents.

Here are some basic guidelines to follow in thinking about your rates. They are not offered as rigid rules. You are free to make your own decisions about whether they will work for your program.

- The fewer hours you work, the more you should charge for your time. Your drop-in rate should be more than your hourly rate. Your hourly rate should be more than your daily rate. Your daily rate should be more than your weekly rate, and your weekly rate should be more than your monthly rate. Why? It's much more difficult for you to manage your time and make ends meet if parents aren't bringing their child every day or every week. Here is a sample rate schedule that follows this model:

Drop-in care (not on a regular basis): $4.00 per hour

Hourly care: $3.50 per hour

Daily care: $3.35 per hour

Weekly care (55 hours a week): $170 per week ($3.09 per hour)

Monthly care (242 hours a month): $665.50 per month ($2.75 per hour)

- Charge by the week or month rather than by the hour. Most providers offer their services for at least eleven hours a day, five days a week. If a parent fails to show up with a child one day, you still have to care for the other children. Parents are paying you to be available to care for their child every day whether they use your services or not. Parents pay for plenty of other services they don't use all of the time (such as health club memberships, apartment rent, magazine and newspaper subscriptions, cable television, and insurance, to name a few).

- Charge parents for days their child is absent due to illness, a parent's vacation, or a federal holiday. Most parents work for employers that offer paid time off for such days. Providers need time off to relax and spend time with their own families. Most child care centers charge for such days.

- Require the client to pay up-front. Do not provide care unless you have already been paid for it. When you first open your home, ask clients to pay for the first week in advance. If clients currently pay you on Friday for that week of care, here's how to get paid in advance. Clients can continue to pay you on Friday. Ask them to pay you for an extra week's worth of care. If they can't afford to pay this all at once, spread out the payment for the extra week until it is affordable. Most clients could afford to pay an additional five dollars a week until the extra week is paid up. Once you get the extra week of payment, clients continue to pay you on Friday, but they are actually paying you for the next week. If clients pay you by the hour, calculate an average weekly payment and ask them to pay this amount up-front. If necessary, spread out the payments. Low-income clients who receive subsidies from the government do not control when payments are made. Ask these clients to pay their own copayment (if any) up-front. Offer payment terms if necessary. Advance payments enable you to cover the cost of food and supplies for the week.

- Establish a consistent time for payment: the day of the week or month and the hour of the day. Set up each client on a payment schedule and stick to it. If a client wants to pay on a Thursday because of family circumstances, and this is acceptable to you, consider agreeing to this. Clients are more likely to pay on time on a regular basis if the payment schedule fits their needs. You can set up different schedules for different customers.

- Require clients to pay for their last two weeks of care up-front. When clients announce they are leaving, their advance payment entitles them to two free weeks of care, even if your rates have risen since they enrolled. You do not have to pay interest to the clients on such advance payments. If a client can't afford to pay this all at once, spread payments over a number of weeks or months. Ask clients on a subsidy program to pay up-front for two weeks of their copayment (if any). Such a policy ensures that you will not be denied payment if a client decides to leave without giving you proper notice.

- Consider raising your rates for infants rather than raising your rates across the board. Infant care is in the greatest demand, and family child care providers are more likely to offer high-quality care for infants than many child care centers. In most areas, however, family child care providers charge significantly less than child care centers. Providers may not realize that parents will pay a lot more for infant care. Some providers don't think infants are more work than older children. Some providers don't raise their rates regularly and, thus, fall behind what centers charge. Call your child care resource and referral (CCR&R) agency to find out how your infant rate compares with other homes and centers.

- Are your rates for infants the same as your rates for preschoolers, or do your rates go down as the child grows older? There is no common policy on this question. Here are some comments that I've heard from providers about charging less as the child grows older:

— "Babies are harder to care for."

— "Everyone else in my area does it. I'd love to change to a set weekly rate, but I don't think parents would stick around if I did."

— "Infants require a lot of equipment and more direct attention and are a higher risk."

— "I can only care for two infants, and infant care is in high demand."

• Here are some reasons why providers charge the same rates regardless of age:

— "Every age has its challenges."

— "I feel that a two- or three-year-old is still taking up a spot just like a six-month-old, so why charge less for older children?"

— "Babies do require extra care, but as a child gets older, she needs more interaction. Older children eat more food and tend to break toys more frequently."

There is no right or wrong way to charge for your services. One provider who charged the same rate said, "I have done this for years but have no idea as to why!"

• Consider charging a fee for other services you provide, such as a late fee, late-payment fee, registration fee, holding fee, or activity fee. A late fee reimburses you for overtime work. A late-payment fee reimburses you for not getting your money on time. A registration fee pays you for the time spent screening parent calls and interviews. A holding fee pays for your promise not to fill a space with another child. An activity fee pays admission and transportation costs for field trips and curriculum costs at home. Sometimes parents just compare weekly or hourly rates when choosing a child care program. Charging separately for these items may make it easier for you to appear more competitive. If you do not charge separately for these fees, make sure you point this out to prospective clients.

• However child care providers charge for their services, they tend not to raise their rates much from year to year. Raise your rates every year. Put this policy in your written contract. Providers traditionally resist annual rate increases, and as a result their profit goes down as other costs increase. Raise your rates regularly even if the amount each year is small. Centers typically raise their rates annually.

- Consider periodically adding paid days to cover your time when you are closed because of sickness, training conferences, or a vacation.

All of these ideas aside, know that we live in a society that does not provide enough public support for young children. When children are old enough to attend first grade, our tax system offers free education. When students enter a college or university, the cost of postsecondary education is heavily subsidized by government, corporations, and private foundations. In contrast, there are few tax subsidies to help parents pay for preschool education. As a result, many parents have a difficult time paying for high-quality care, and many providers have a difficult time supporting themselves on what parents can afford to pay. Until there is more public support for young children, it will always be hard for providers to earn a living commensurate with the value of the service they deliver to society. Although providers should continue to press for the best possible rates from parents, they should also be advocates in the public policy arena to seek a more equitable child care financing system. The best way to do this is by joining with local, state, and national advocacy organizations. For more information, see appendix M, "Additional Resources."

Credit/Debit Cards and Electronic Payments

Some providers have started accepting credit or debit cards as forms of payment for their services. Offering this service may make child care payments more convenient for parents, which means you are more likely to receive payments on time. The disadvantage is that there is often a cost associated with processing card payments. To get more information, talk to your local bank.

Many providers now use electronic payment systems to receive parent payments. Several companies provide such services, including Reliafund (www.reliafund.com), Minute Menu Kids Pro (www.minutemenu.com), and Novera Payment Solutions (www.noverapaymentsolutions.com/nafcc). You may also be able to set up an electronic payment plan through your local bank. With this kind of system, parents agree to have funds electronically withdrawn from their bank account and transferred into your bank account. Usually there is a waiting period of a few days before the transaction is completed. Many parents like this system because it means they no longer have to remember their checkbook. Providers like this system because they receive payments more reliably. The drawback is that there is a fee for this service.

What Should You Base Your Rates On?

When you are setting your rates, figure out the amount you want to earn after your business expenses, the going rate in your community (for both child care homes and centers), and the ability of clients to pay. Let's look at each one of these factors in turn.

How Much Do You Want to Earn?

Few providers even think of asking this question, but if you don't set a goal for what you want to earn, your take-home pay probably won't meet your expectations. Take the time to think through this answer. What rate would be too high? That is, what rate would prevent too many parents from enrolling and force you out of business? What rate would be too low? That is, what rate would mean you would not earn enough income to live on? If you are following some of the marketing tips in this book and are communicating the benefits of your program to prospective clients, you probably should be charging at the high end of the going rate in your community. Look at the rates at both center-based and family child care programs in your area when determining the going rate.

Your income goal may be to earn a specific amount of money each year. Or your goal may be to be paid an amount equal to what a teacher at a local child care center earns with the same training and experience as you have. As an example, let's say your goal is to earn $8.00 an hour after business expenses (as of the beginning of 2012, federal minimum wage is $7.25 an hour). Here's how to determine what your rate should be to meet this goal:

1   **Calculate your annual income goal.**

   If you are just starting out as a provider, you probably can expect to care for children about eleven hours a day, five days a week. You can expect to work another ten hours a week doing other business work, such as cleaning, record keeping, and preparing meals. This equals 65 hours a week, or 3,380 hours a year (with a two-week paid vacation). If you have been in business for at least a year, look at line four of your previous year's IRS **Form 8829 Business Use of Your Home**. This represents the total number of hours you said you worked last year. Let's say you have 3,380 hours on this line. Multiply this number by $8 per hour. The total is $27,040. This represents how much you want to earn after paying for business expenses.

2   **Determine your gross income goal.**

   A national survey of family child care providers determined that annual business expenses represent about 37 percent of your income before taxes (see "The Economics of Family Child Care Study," cited in appendix M). Using the numbers in our example, you can estimate your gross-income goal based on your business expenses. If your expenses are 37 percent of your gross income, then your income goal is 63 percent of your gross income (100% − 37% = 63%). So your gross income goal is $42,921 ($27,040 ÷ 63% = $42,921). That means your business expenses are $15,881 ($42,921 − $27,040 = $15,881). Remember, this gross-income goal is just an example. If you have been in business for at least a full year, look at the line titled "Tentative Profit" on your IRS **Schedule C Profit or Loss from Business** (line 29) from last year. This line represents your business profit. We won't include house expenses (such as property taxes, rent, mortgage interest, and so on) in this total, because these would be expenses even if you were not in business. You might want to add to this amount any money you want to set aside for retirement or health insurance. We'll use the $15,881 amount for business expenses for our example.

3   **Establish your weekly child care rate.**

   By dividing the gross income goal of $42,921 by the number of children you care for, you can determine how much you will need to charge per week per child. Here's the breakdown (assuming a two-week paid vacation):

2 children ($42,921 ÷ 2 children ÷ 52 weeks) = $413 per week

3 children ($42,921 ÷ 3 children ÷ 52 weeks) = $275 per week

4 children ($42,921 ÷ 4 children ÷ 52 weeks) = $206 per week

5 children ($42,921 ÷ 5 children ÷ 52 weeks) = $165 per week

6 children ($42,921 ÷ 6 children ÷ 52 weeks) = $138 per week

In this example, to meet your goal of earning $8 an hour for your work, you would have to charge an average of $138 per week if you care for six children and $165 per week if you care for five children. Many providers are currently charging less than these amounts. These numbers would change if you worked fewer or longer hours and if your expenses were different. You would also need to adjust your rate if you charge different rates for different age groups. The example also assumes that you maintain full enrollment for the entire year. See appendix B for a worksheet you can use to calculate your own weekly rate.

Some parents don't like paying for a provider's vacation because they must pay double for the weeks their provider is gone. You may want to offer parents the option of paying a little more each week so they won't have to pay you during the weeks you take your vacations. For example, let's say you are earning $520 per week (65 hours a week x $8 per hour = $520). To be paid for a two-week vacation, you need to earn an extra $1,040 per year. If you care for two children and each parent paid an extra $10.40 per week, you wouldn't need parents to pay you during your two weeks of vacation ($1,040 ÷ 50 weeks ÷ 2 children = $10.40). If you care for three children, each parent would have to pay an extra $6.93 per week ($1,040 ÷ 50 weeks ÷ 3 children = $6.93). For four children, the amount would be $5.20 extra per week; for five children, $4.16; and for six children, $3.47.

Remember, this example is not meant to dictate what your rates should be. It is intended to help you better understand the relationship between your rates and your profit. Eight dollars an hour, although more than what many providers now earn, is still well below what public school teachers—who often have similar training and experience—earn.

If you have been in business for at least a year, here's how you can determine how much you earned per hour last year after business expenses. Take the number from the "Tentative Profit" line near the bottom of your last year's **Schedule C** and divide it by line 4 on your **Form 8829**. In other words, divide your business profit by the number of hours you worked last year. You may be surprised to discover—as many providers would—that you are earning much less than the minimum wage.

What Is the Going Rate in Your Community?

Child care rates tend to fluctuate widely, even in small communities. For this reason, it's probably not a good idea to pay close attention to the "average" rate in your area. Your local CCR&R agency or government subsidy agency can tell you the average rate. Ask them when the most recent survey was conducted. If the survey is more than six months old, you may want to assume that current rates are probably a little higher. Make sure you look at the range of rates to give you a better idea of what clients are paying. Find out the range for the highest 20 percent of rates and then the next 20 percent. This will tell you a lot. For example, let's say these are the weekly rates in your area for infant care in family child care homes:

Top 20%: $250, $210, $210, $200, $190, $190, $150, $145, $145, $145, $140, $140, $140, $140

Next 20%: $135, $135, $130, $130, $130, $125, $125, $125, $125, $125, $125, $125, $125

This tells us that most of these providers charge between $125 and $150 a week, but there are six providers who charge significantly more. Find out who these providers are and how they are able to charge these rates. Maybe these providers have high fees but enroll very few infants. Or maybe they operate a well-organized, high-quality program that specializes in infant care. These providers simply might have decided to charge higher rates and found their clients were willing to pay them. Compare your program to the programs in these two groups to see where you fall. Because the cost of child care varies widely from one part of the country to another, the rates in this example may not be appropriate for your neighborhood.

Now look at the rates for infant care at the child care centers in your area. There are probably fewer centers to gather data from. Just survey the nearby centers that are likely to be your competition. Your CCR&R agency may have this rate information. Examine these centers to see how their service compares with yours. Are you offering as many benefits? Don't hesitate to compare the quality of your program with that of child care centers.

Conduct the same market research as outlined for toddler, preschool, and school-age care.

What Can Clients Afford to Pay?

This is the most difficult factor to measure. Look at the upper end of what clients can afford to pay. After doing so, you may decide to set your rates higher than what some clients will pay; there is no rule that says you must set your rates low enough so no parent will be denied service. Whether you want to keep your rates affordable to low-income parents is your decision. Most businesses operate knowing that some customers will not buy their service because of the price. Here are some tips on how to attract and serve higher-income parents:

- Offer a special service that few other providers offer. This might mean taking extended field trips or offering music lessons. If clients can't get your special service anywhere else, you should be charging a premium price for it.

- The hours you provide care are the most valuable commodities of your business. Consider offering odd-hour care, weekend care, or drop-in care to meet client demand. Ask your local CCR&R agency what hours are in demand but difficult for parents to find. When a service is scarce, the price for that service should go up.

- Focus on any unique benefits you currently provide and use them to justify your higher rates. You might say, "I speak Spanish, which exposes children to a second language that will help them succeed in school."

- If you have never lost a client because of high rates, your rates are probably too low. While you can't expect clients to be happy when you raise your rates, know that many more providers have gone out of business because their rates were too low than because they were too high.

- It will probably take more time to find parents who are willing to pay a higher rate for your services. Plan the timeline for your marketing efforts accordingly. Your efforts will need to take place over a longer period before you will see results.

- Run ads and distribute business flyers in neighborhoods where higher-income parents live. Your business name and the design of your marketing materials should be more professional and less folksy. You may want to promote your program as having a preschool curriculum, describe yourself as a teacher, and charge parents tuition. Consider modeling some of the ways child care centers create a professional relationship with parents.

- Many providers complain that the only thing clients care about is price, but this idea is probably a myth. Parents continue to enroll their children in child care centers, which usually charge higher rates than family child care homes. A 2008 survey by the National Association for Child Care Resource and Referral Agencies (NACCRRA) found that the cost of care was the third most important factor for parents when choosing child care. Finding a safe environment and finding a learning environment with learning activities were the two most important factors (see *Parents' Perceptions of Child Care in the United States*, cited in appendix M).

- Clients are less likely to pay attention to rates when the following circumstances are true:

  — You charge within an expected price range for child care services when compared with other homes and centers. Unless your rates are at the very high end of those in your community, this is probably true for you.

  — You offer a service that is valuable at almost any price. Certainly child care meets this definition.

  — The service you offer is desperately needed. This is probably true for infant care and evening care. It is less true for preschool care. Because preschool care is in much greater supply, the price for this service is more competitive and clients will do more price shopping.

  — It is difficult for parents to compare your service with their other options. There is little information available to help clients adequately compare one child care program with another. Therefore, parents are less price conscious.

— It is hard to find substitutes for your service. Parents can look in the Yellow Pages and find a child care center easily. With other options available, price becomes more important.

— Your care seems inexpensive to clients. This is probably not true for most clients.

Most of the preceding statements are true for child care, which should mean that parents are not as price sensitive as you might think. Shouldn't parents expect to pay more for child care in a home environment, where there are fewer children and a consistent caregiver who is trained in how to care for children of different ages? Of course.

According to a 2002 study, resistance to higher rates often comes from the child care provider, not the parent. The study found that providers were reluctant to raise fees because they feared parents could not afford to pay more, despite the fact that the providers reported no vacancies and had waiting lists. This suggests that providers base their fees on what they consider to be a fair price rather than on what would maximize their income (see "Family Child Care Finances and Their Effect on Quality and Incentives" by Suzanne W. Helburn, John R. Morris, and Kathy Modigliani, *Early Childhood Research Quarterly* 17 [4]). This report also found that for each year of additional education a provider achieved, her fees increased an average of three dollars a week.

Talking to Parents about Raising Rates

This is probably one of the most difficult conversations you will have with your clients. Here are some suggestions that might help:

- If you decide to raise your rates, notify clients at least one month in advance. This is no time to surprise them.
- Don't raise your rates in April (when tax bills are due) or in December (when holiday expenses can be a burden).
- September is generally a good time to raise rates, because this is often when children begin school and when you will need to fill an opening.

- Raise your rates for new clients only, and keep rates steady for current clients. There is no law that prevents you from charging different rates to different clients based on when the client enrolled. If you do charge different rates, however, assume that your clients will eventually find out what others are paying. As long as you can justify the different rates, you should be fine.

- Don't raise everyone's rates at the same time. If you do, you run the risk of losing more than one parent at the same time. Stagger rate increases so only one family at a time is affected. You may want to pick the client's anniversary date as the time to raise rates. Some providers regularly raise their rates for all clients every January or September without any problems.

- Instead of raising rates, charge annual fees for liability insurance, attendance at a family child care conference, NAFCC accreditation fees, or other special expenses.

- Don't overjustify your rate increase. No matter what you say, some parent may not agree with your reasoning. Just announce your new rates in writing. If clients ask for an explanation, consider telling them the following:

    — "My costs have gone up (such as for utilities, property tax, or food)."

    — "It is a cost-of-living raise."

    — "I have another year of experience in providing care, and I've applied this knowledge to help your child learn more."

    — "I have introduced a new benefit to my program (such as a computer, extra field trips, or a new curriculum)."

    — "I have taken additional training workshops in the past year, and this enables me to do a better job of caring for your child."

    — "I am working longer hours to care for children or to prepare for activities."

    — "I am providing certain special services that are not common."

    — "I will be providing better care for your child this coming year because _____ (fill in your explanation)."

- Sometimes clients look at what they pay you each week, multiply it by how many other children are in your care, and conclude that you are making a lot of money. They don't realize all the expenses you have in running your business. To better understand your business, you might want to prepare an income and expense chart like the one that follows. Lump the business expenses from your tax return into five or six categories as a percentage of your total income. This chart is based on data collected from family child care providers in three cities (see "The Economics of Family Child Care Study," cited in appendix M).

Income	Average (1992)
Parent fees	90%
Food Program	10%
Total gross income	100%
Expenses	
Food	35%
Employees, insurance	26%
Supplies, toys	17%
Professional fees/other	10%
Maintenance/repairs/equipment	7%
Transportation/gifts	5%
Total expenses	100% (37% of gross income)
Profit	63% of gross income

Note: The expenses do not include taxes or house expenses (such as property taxes, mortgage interest, and so on) that existed before the business began.

This chart shows that the average provider in this study kept only sixty-three cents on every dollar of income earned. Your financial chart may be very different. The point is that most providers must spend a lot of money on business expenses to operate successfully. When you are thinking about how much money you are making, you should always be looking at your profit *after* business expenses. You may want to share some of the information on your own financial chart with your customers to help educate them about your business. You might want to share only a couple of expense categories, such as food and supplies/toys. You don't want to share this information as the sole justification for your rates, but many parents will be surprised at how much you must spend to stay in business.

- Don't argue with clients who say your rates are too high. They may be too high for the particular client you are talking to. You may want to mention ways your fees could be considered more affordable, such as by pointing out the benefits of the federal child care tax credit, child and dependent care assistance plans, any discounts you offer for second children, or any other special discounts you might offer.

- Your best way of communicating about your rates is to talk about the *value* of your service rather than the price. The cost of providing quality child care is expensive. Parents can always find cheaper care somewhere else. Point out to parents how your program benefits their child and mention that your rate takes these benefits into account. Clients will pay more if they can see the value of your benefits and the quality of your service.

- Parents sometimes believe that if child care costs more, it must be worth it. Years ago, a parent called a CCR&R agency looking for infant care. After getting several names from the referral counselor, the parent asked, "Which provider charges the most?" The counselor started to explain that he should check out all the providers and compare their services, when the parent interrupted to say, "You don't understand. I want to know who charges the most, because I think that provider will offer the best care." Parents, like many consumers, believe that they get what they pay for. Parents generally pay more to enroll their child in a child care center because they believe they are getting higher-quality care. In part, this belief is based on the higher rates charged by centers. If you charge less than a center but claim that the quality of your care is better, some parents may wonder why you aren't charging more. When you price your work, you price your worth.

- Parents are reluctant to change child care providers and are more likely to pay you an additional amount than be inconvenienced by the need to search for another provider.

Hotels and Family Child Care

When I conduct workshops on marketing, I like to use the following exercise to illustrate how family child care providers should think about their rates.

First I give the providers a scenario. I tell them, "Let's say we all have to stay overnight at a hotel or motel in a medium-sized city. We'd probably have close to a hundred choices to choose from. Let's say we call all of the hotels and ask about their benefits ('Why should I stay at your hotel tonight?') and their price. Then we put the names of the hotels on a large notepad, listing them in order of price, with the most expensive hotel at the top of the list and the cheapest at the bottom."

I then ask the group, "How many of you would stay at the cheapest hotel in town?" Usually very few providers, if any, raise their hand. I ask, "Why not? What are you willing to pay more for in a hotel?" The answers come quickly: safety, a free breakfast, an exercise room, cleanliness, the location, an on-site restaurant, a swimming pool, and so on.

Now I change the rules and say to the providers, "Let's say that we have only two choices for where to spend the night. The first choice is the ABC Hotel and the second choice is the XYZ Hotel. They are located right next to each other, and they have the exact same benefits. Which one do you choose?" The correct answer from the audience is, "The cheaper one."

What does this exercise tell us? Child care providers shop for hotels the same way we all shop for items in our daily lives—which is the same way parents shop for child care. If we are shopping for shoes, we are willing to pay more for a pair that has more benefits (that is, higher-quality shoes), according to what we believe is a benefit (such as color, style, shape, and so on). If the shoes seem to have the same benefits, we'll look at price and buy the cheaper one.

Unfortunately, this normal shopping behavior doesn't work well when parents shop for child care. Parents who are looking for child care, particularly family child care, often cannot see the difference in benefits from one provider to another. This is because providers generally do not clearly communicate their benefits. Ask any group of providers to list three benefits of their program, and you'll probably see them struggle to answer quickly and clearly. Since child care programs often look the same to parents (that is, they appear to have the same benefits), parents are often left to make a child care decision based on the only distinguishing feature: price.

This is a tragedy for the child care field, where quality and price cannot be easily matched in the same way as most other products (such as hotels and shoes). In my opinion, the best child care providers in any town are not necessarily the ones charging the most money. This is a terrible situation because it confuses customers who are looking for a high-quality program. These customers can't use price as a measure, but they also can't identify any other measure of quality because providers communicate their benefits poorly. If you are a provider who thinks parents are only interested in your price, you may not be clearly distinguishing between the benefits of your program compared with other child care programs in your area.

Think about it this way. Let's say a provider in your town offers high-quality care and does a great job of communicating her benefits, but she charges no more than the average rate in town. Because her rates don't reflect it, she is sending a message to parents that she doesn't really offer high-quality care. Remember the example I shared of the father who was looking for the most expensive care in town because he assumed that would be the highest-quality care? Ultimately, the providers who do the best job of offering high-quality care and communicating their benefits are the providers who will attract parents, charge the highest rates, and stay in business longer.

Even if one of your clients is a relative or someone who was a friend before enrolling with you, everything in this chapter about setting rates still applies, Although you have a personal relationship with relatives and friends, you must establish a business relationship when dealing with money. You should clearly set out your rate schedule and enforce it in the same way you would with any client. If it feels too uncomfortable to be in a business relationship with a relative or friend, then you should reconsider what you are doing. You may feel more comfortable providing care for free, or you may decide that you would rather not provide the care at all.

In the end, you deserve to be paid as a professional provider who is doing the important work of teaching young children and helping them develop into adults. You are worth it!

CHAPTER 10

Other Marketing Issues

This chapter addresses some additional issues that may arise when marketing your family child care business.

Competing against Child Care Centers

A new child care center just opened in your neighborhood. It offers care for a hundred children (toddler through school-age) and has a well-equipped playground, a van to transport children, and sparkling classrooms with bright furniture and plenty of toys. You start to feel desperate, wondering if you'll ever be able to fill your two openings. "How can I compete?" you ask.

In some ways, child care centers have an advantage over family child care. They are easier to find, they have a full staff, their buildings are easily accessible to the public, and they can spend money on advertising. Some parents are afraid to use family child care providers because providers are alone in their home, and parents worry about what goes on behind closed doors. For these reasons, providers need to work hard to counteract parents' fears. Here are some suggestions:

- Visit your local child care center and get copies of all materials the staff distributes to prospective clients, such as rate schedules, statements of philosophy, and descriptions of benefits, special services, and time-limited special discounts. Watch for any advertisements for the center in local newspapers or magazines or in flyers distributed in the neighborhood. (See page 170 about how to collect this information without violating antitrust laws.) You want to keep monitoring what this center is doing. Prospective clients who call you may be comparing what you offer with what this center offers, so you need to be informed.

• Look over all the materials you have collected. Think about how your program is different from the center. Look at your benefits. What do you offer that the center does not? Your answer might include some of these benefits:

— a smaller group size, which allows for more individual attention

— a home environment where children can play in familiar, comfortable surroundings

— home-cooked, individually prepared meals

— a healthier environment for children because fewer illnesses are spread in a small group

— a more convenient location

— less expensive rates (Some providers may want to promote this as a benefit, but readers of this book should understand by now that many providers can successfully compete on the basis of the quality of their care rather than on lower rates.)

— longer or more flexible hours

— years of experience

— a consistent caregiver (Staff turnover at centers is usually high, resulting in a less stable relationship between caregiver and child.)

— mixed age groups, allowing siblings to be together

— transportation to and from school, or a school bus stopping at your home

— credentials or accreditation

Remember, your program may never have everything a center offers, but you will always have some benefits that a center does not have. See chapter 2 for a description of how to identify the benefits of your program.

- Call your child care resources and referral (CCR&R) agency and ask what type of care is in great demand in your neighborhood. You may want to adjust your program to offer second-shift or weekend care, or you may want to focus on caring for children with special needs or of different ages than you are currently caring for.

- In your neighborhood, distribute door hangers and business flyers that describe your program, identify its key benefits, and offer a discount on the first month of care.

- Offer current clients a finder's fee if they refer a parent who enrolls with you.

- Work with your local family child care association to run advertisements in neighborhood newspapers. The ad should promote family child care and give a phone number to call for referrals to homes in your neighborhood.

- Introduce yourself to the director of the center. Suggest ways you might cooperate. If this center doesn't offer infant care and you do, ask if the center will refer parents with infants to you (or to your family child care association's referral service). Offer to provide backup care for the center for mildly ill children. If the center closes at 6:00 p.m., offer to provide drop-in care for clients who need care until 7:00 p.m.

Competing against Informal Caregivers

Providers who run their business outside of the regulatory system are popping up everywhere. These providers are exempt from regulations because they either care for only a few children or are operating illegally. The best way to compete against illegal providers is to turn them in to your local government regulators or to the IRS (see pages 127–28). But what can you do about the increasing number of providers who, while not operating illegally, nonetheless operate without having to follow all of the regulations you do?

- Parents' number one concern about child care is safety. Therefore, you should emphasize to parents that being regulated means you and your program have passed a series of safety tests, including criminal background checks on all adults in the home, first aid and CPR training, fire department inspections of your home, and adherence to safety standards, such as properly storing hazardous materials around the home. Parents who use an informal caregiver must check out these things for themselves to ensure their child's safety.

- Informal caregivers probably charge less, perhaps significantly less, than you charge. Do not compete on the basis of price by lowering your rates. There will always be providers with lower rates than yours, and you can be successful without undercutting your competition. Think of the hotel exercise in chapter 9 (see page 161). There are cheap hotels and expensive hotels. They all compete in different ways to attract customers. As a reader of this book, you should probably not see yourself as a Motel 6 or Super 8. How about an Embassy Suites or a Sheraton?

- Compete against informal caregivers by stressing the value of your services. Do this by promoting the benefits of your program as described in chapter 2. What advantages do you offer to children and parents who enroll with your regulated program? Your answer might include the following:

  — "I offer a variety of planned learning and play activities that will help your child be ready to succeed academically and socially in school."

  — "I have a backup caregiver who can provide care if I am ever sick or gone, so you won't miss work."

  — "I have specialized training in child development, so I can respond quickly to your child's needs."

  — "I offer special services (such as piano lessons, second-language training, numerous field trips, or computers) that will enrich your child's education."

- If clients can see that you provide high-quality care, they are likely to pay more for it. You can't appeal to everyone. Some parents will always pick the cheapest care. Let those parents go. People usually get what they pay for. Parents who pay bargain-basement rates will get bargain-basement care.

- Work with your family child care association or CCR&R agency to initiate a public education campaign about the benefits of regulated child care. Direct this campaign at both parents and informal caregivers. To parents, stress the issues of safety, training, and professional care. To informal caregivers, stress the benefits of the Food Program, access to support, and the ability to earn more money by caring for more children. See appendix L, "Tax Benefits of Becoming a Regulated Family Child Care Provider," for more information.

Marketing during Financial Hard Times

Marketing a child care business is never easy, even when the economy is doing well. So when the economy isn't doing well, marketing is extremely difficult. Parents lose their jobs and take their children out of child care. Some of these parents start caring for the children of their neighbors as a way to make ends meet while they look for work outside the home. Thus, the demand for care drops at the same time the supply of care increases. How can you respond to this dilemma? Here are some suggestions:

- Be flexible about your holding fee. Let's say a parent plans to enroll in your program a few months in advance of when she needs care, but she is reluctant to pay your holding fee. You don't want to lose this client, so you may want to tell her, "I'll keep looking to fill the space I have in my program. If I don't find anyone to enroll by the time you need care, you will be able to enroll without paying any holding fee. If I do find someone to enroll before you need care, I'll call you and let you know that you can hold your spot if you pay me a small holding fee at that time." Because it's more difficult to fill spaces during economic hard times, you are less likely to be able to fill your space before the parent needs care. You won't lose the parent, and the parent won't have to pay a holding fee.

- Resist the temptation to lower your rates during a recession. You may want to offer temporary discounts or incentive coupons to attract new clients, but lowering your rates is generally a bad idea. Remember, you can compete with other programs even if you don't have the cheapest rate in town.

Let's say, for example, a parent wants to enroll her child in your program, but she is concerned that she can't quite afford your rates. You may want to offer a temporary discount for one to six months to get her in your door. Hopefully, after some months have passed, the parent will be in a better financial situation and will want to stay in your program because of your high-quality care. It's not illegal to lower your rates (temporarily) for a new client while keeping your rates higher for existing families. If an existing parent is concerned that she is paying more than a new parent, explain that you offered a temporary discount.

- Be flexible. A provider once called me with a question about how to handle a situation with one of her parents. This provider only cared for children of teachers, so she closed her program during the summer. A parent in her program was hurting financially and asked if she could pay less during the school year and make up the difference during the summer. The provider didn't want to lose this client and didn't mind losing some income during the school year in exchange for being paid the difference later. I thought it was a good idea for the provider to keep this family in her program, and I urged her to change her contract to state that if either party ended the contract before the end of summer, the parent would pay any money still due.

- Raise your finder's fee. The increase will appeal to families who are also suffering financially. The incentive may cause them to work harder to help you fill your spaces. Again, instituting a finder's fee creates positive word of mouth, and you don't have to pay anything out of pocket until you receive income from the new family.

- Give parents a reason for staying in your program. Since losing a family during an economic downturn can be painful, do everything you can to keep current parents from leaving. Take a close look at the suggestions in chapter 4, and institute several of the ideas over the course of the year. One provider, for example, normally charges a minimal fee for her "Parents' Night Out" service, an evening of care once a month (during which she serves the children pizza and snacks) so parents can go out. During a recession, she offers this as a free service because it helps create good word of mouth.

When recessions occur, some states cut back on the financial assistance programs that help low-income parents pay for child care. In response, some states raise parent copays or drop parents entirely from the program. When this happens, family child care providers end up in a serious bind. Providers are faced with uncomfortable choices: they can raise rates on low-income families, drop them from their program, or continue to provide care for a reduced fee or no fee. For providers who care for a substantial number of subsidized families, this creates an even more serious problem that can drive some providers out of business. Let's look more closely at the consequences of these choices:

- Let's say you decide to charge low-income parents your regular rate (or raise your copayment fee). Some or many of these families may not be able to afford the expense and may be forced to leave your program.

- Let's say you decide to offer part-time care or odd-hour care at a reduced price to enable these parents to use your program for at least a few hours each week. Doing so may allow parents to keep their children in your program, but your income will be lower.

- Let's say you decide to continue caring for the child but accept less than your full pay. Some child care providers give parents a "scholarship." Whatever you call it (a "scholarship" or "discount" or something else), you cannot deduct the amount of free care that you deliver as a business expense. You will report less income on your tax return and pay less in taxes as a result, but free care is never deductible.

There are no easy answers for how to handle state cutbacks to child care subsidy programs. It's a time when many child care providers try to do what they can to help out these families, even if it means accepting less money for their work. Whether or not you decide to help out in this way, I support your efforts to offer quality care for all children, regardless of parent income.

Price Fixing: Collecting Information about Rates

What do the following situations have in common?

- At an association meeting or training workshop, family child care providers discuss how much they charge clients.

- In order to find out the going rate in her neighborhood, a new provider calls another provider and asks what she charges clients.

- A family child care association surveys its members about rates and shares the results at the next association meeting.

In all of the above situations, there is a probable violation of federal antitrust laws. What's going on?

Federal antitrust laws restrict competitors from discussing their rates with each other. The law is meant to encourage competition and to discourage competitors from setting prices higher than they would be otherwise. When providers discuss rates at association meetings or training workshops, this can easily be construed as a discussion to raise rates. This is true even when no direct statements are made to encourage providers to raise rates.

Many providers and family child care trainers are not aware of how federal anti-trust laws affect the family child care field. Although these laws are violated regularly when providers discuss rates over the phone, providers should be most concerned when the issue of rates comes up at association meetings or training workshops. Many years ago, a family child care association in Minnesota got in trouble for dis-cussing rates at an orientation for new providers. Someone complained to the state attorney general's office, and after the investigation was over, the association officers signed a letter promising never to do it again and agreeing to pay a $10,000 fine if it ever happened again.

At the same time, being informed about what other programs (homes and centers) charge is important. This information can be used to help you market your program. If you are charging more than other providers, you can promote the value of your benefits that justify a higher rate. Just be careful about how you use the rate information you do collect. If your rates are higher than average in your area, don't assume you must lower your rates to be competitive. Don't assume that you shouldn't raise your rates either. Your rates should be based on what you want to earn and the cost of doing business; see chapter 9 for more information.

How can you collect rate information without breaking the law? If you call another provider or visit a child care center, don't identify yourself as a provider. Both parties must know they are competitors for the conversation to be price fixing. Instead, say you are a parent looking for child care and you want to know what local rates are. Or ask a friend to visit the center, collect information about rates, and bring it back to you. You can also ask parents what they paid past providers or what their friends pay for child care. As another option, look at classified ads (print and online), Craigslist ads, and business flyers posted in your neighborhood to see what other providers are charging. It's legal to make your own rates public through such forums.

For more comprehensive information, call your local CCR&R agency or local government child care subsidy program and ask for any rate information that has been collected. Many CCR&R agencies and government agencies conduct regular surveys of provider rates (homes and centers). As a provider, you can ask for this information without fear of breaking the law. Rate information can be shared if it meets these three conditions:

1   The individual or organization collects the rate information and makes it readily available to the public.

2   The information is communicated in a way that doesn't allow anyone to identify the rates of individual providers.

3   The sample of providers surveyed is large enough so no one can identify the name of any one provider.

Usually, CCR&R and government agencies collect only minimal information about rates (the average cost of care by age group, for example). Ask the agency to collect additional information that is more useful, such as the range of rates for the following categories of providers:

- providers whose rates fall among the lowest third, middle third, and highest third

- providers open less than two years

- providers open more than ten years
- providers who are members of the association
- providers who have a CDA or are NAFCC accredited
- providers in a geographical area close to your home

In addition, ask the agency to find out the percentage of providers who charge for the following (and to find out the range of costs for each one):

- provider vacation
- parent vacation
- registration fee
- activity fee
- late-pickup fee
- late-payment fee
- bounced-check fee
- second-child discount
- holding fee (such as during maternity leave and summer break)

If the CCR&R or government agency surveys providers for this information and shares it with the public (which includes parents who call looking for child care), then individual providers can receive it.

Members of family child care associations should also be concerned about how they collect rate information. Associations that operate a referral service for parents and collect specific rate information from members can give this information to parents who call, but they cannot share this information with other providers in the association. If your family child care association wants to collect rate information from members, it must follow the three conditions identified on the previous page. That means the association would need to have someone other than a provider (who is a competitor) collect the information.

In addition to passing out the rate information to parents, the association could calculate the average rates for its members and make this information available to the public. This could be done by sharing the results with local CCR&R and government agencies or by publishing the results in local parenting magazines. By sharing average rate information with the public, association members could then have access to this data. Associations can always share rate information collected by a CCR&R or government agencies with its own members. For more information about price fixing, see the *Family Child Care Legal and Insurance Guide*.

How Can I Afford to Pay for Marketing?

Marketing your business doesn't have to be an elaborate campaign or cost a lot of money. But a successful business will have to spend some money on marketing. Many of the ideas in this book are very inexpensive. Plan to spend a few dollars on your marketing efforts each month. Remember that all of your marketing expenses are 100 percent tax deductible.

What follows is a list of the top ten low-cost marketing tips for your business. If you are just starting out or need to fill an opening and don't have much money, try these ideas first. If you follow all ten ideas, you can expect to spend less than $200 a year, or about $15 a month. The costs below are estimates. They will vary in different parts of the country.

Top Ten Low-Cost Marketing Tips and Estimated Costs

1	Choose a name for your business and register it with your state (see pages 75–77).	$30
2	Print 250 business cards listing your name and phone number. Distribute your cards to friends, relatives, neighbors, and others. Vistaprint (www.vistaprint.com) offers free business cards (see pages 77–78).	$15
3	Create a one-page flyer about your business. Identify three things about your program that are special and put them in your flyer. Print and distribute one hundred copies at local businesses, churches, and schools (see pages 82–84).	$25
4	Record a friendly and professional greeting on your answering machine or voice mail that identifies your business and invites parents to leave a message (see pages 25–27).	Free

5   Place a four-line classified ad on an online classified ad service
(see pages 101–104). $25

6   Talk to your local CCR&R agency about being a part of its referral
service. Ask a referral counselor for tips on how to attract clients
(see pages 113–17).   Free

7   Join your local family child care association and take advantage of its
member benefits (see pages 120–24). $25

8   Offer a finder's fee to anyone who refers a parent to you or who enrolls
and stays at least three months (see pages 58–59). $50

9   Create an inviting and safe first impression for parents by cleaning up
the outside of your home and your entryway (see pages 24–25).   Free

10 When a parent calls about your program, make sure you follow up
with a thank-you note and a return call to try and schedule an interview
(see page 39).   45¢

Total Estimated Cost	**$170.45**

CHAPTER 11

Evaluating Your Plan

Child care is a dynamic service industry that has just come of age as a profession. Marketing is a year-round, ongoing process. Here are some final tips to help you with your marketing efforts:

- Marketing should be fun! Promoting your business shouldn't always be an overly serious activity. Try to laugh at yourself as much as possible and have a good time when you are marching in a local parade, writing notes on Facebook or your blog, throwing a holiday or Halloween party, passing out balloons, or writing the next issue of your newsletter. If you do not enjoy your business activities, consider finding a profession that will make you happy.

- Marketing requires attention over the long run. Pace yourself. Don't conduct six marketing activities the first month and then nothing for the next eight months. See appendix A, "Annual Marketing Calendar," for ideas about how to schedule your activities.

- All of your marketing activities should support each other and present a consistent message to clients. You should continually promote the benefits of your program. The benefits should appear consistently in all of your written materials (such as your business flyer, classified ad, door hanger, and website). Use the same color and design on all your marketing materials.

- All of the marketing tips in this book should work together to help define your program. You may have a brilliant business flyer, but if your telephone manner is unfriendly, parents will turn away. You may be very successful in enrolling new clients, but if you can't communicate with clients about their needs, you probably won't keep them for long.

- Don't rely on any single marketing idea to fill your openings, and don't assume that you only need to tell parents about your program once. You will probably have to use several marketing strategies several times before a potential customer will listen.

- Try not to become overwhelmed by the many ideas in this book. Pick out a few to get started. And don't be afraid to try your own ideas.

- At least once a year, take time to evaluate your marketing plan. In reviewing your efforts, ask yourself the following questions:

  — What am I doing to keep my current clients happy?

  — How well is it working?

  — What ideas for my program have current clients suggested that I can implement now?

- Look at your current clients and see if you can identify any similarities, such as in where they live, their ages, jobs, and lifestyles. How did they hear about you? Knowing this information may help you focus your marketing efforts for the coming year. Consider the following questions as well:

  — How did parents who call me hear about me? Which marketing ideas worked? What other ideas should I try now? What ideas are working for other providers?

  — How many parents who contacted me ended up enrolling in my program? Why didn't more enroll?

  — How many parents stayed with me? How many parents left in the past year? Did I provide all of the benefits I said I would in my marketing materials?

  — What advice do child care resource and referral agencies, family child care associations, and child care regulators have to offer me?

  — What can I learn this year from my competitors?

- For some providers, marketing can be stressful. If you are feeling anxious, take a step back and don't initiate any new marketing activities for a while. To help avoid burnout, take a Friday off or take a vacation. Seek help from a support group or a mentor. There will always be times when you need some extra help to reduce your stress level.

- Be patient. Few marketing efforts produce instant results. It takes time to build a successful business.

- Appreciate yourself. Be proud of your commitment to help young children. Your work is important, and you shouldn't feel shy about promoting what you do. If you decide that you can't meet your business goals and have to quit, don't be discouraged. Your business may have failed, but you have not. As long as you have a positive attitude about yourself, you will succeed.

Appendixes

Annual Marketing Calendar

Marketing is a year-round activity. Don't try to squeeze all of your efforts into a few months. Try to maintain a steady stream of activities each month. The cumulative effect of your marketing will grow over time. Here's a sample list of marketing tasks spread throughout the year. You can follow this schedule or establish your own. Post your schedule where you will see it regularly, such as in your office.

January

- Call your CCR&R agency to make sure your listing is correct and to talk to a referral counselor about parent demand.
- Offer current clients a finder's fee if they refer a parent with a preschooler to your program who stays enrolled for at least three months.
- Fill out the IRS **Form W-10** and give a copy to each parent. Have the parent sign a year-end receipt for last year's child care payments. Mail a copy of the **W-10** to parents who left your program earlier in the year. Send past clients a copy of your business flyer.

February

- Identify three benefits of your program. Post them next to each of your phones.
- Register your business name with your state.
- Give your current families a Valentine's Day card and a note of appreciation.

March

- Print business cards and distribute at least thirty to friends and neighbors.
- Record a new greeting on your answering machine.
- Start a Facebook page for your business.

April

- If you know that you'll lose a toddler when a parent moves out of town in June, call your CCR&R agency to tell them you will have an opening for a toddler soon.
- At your family child care association meeting, ask for the names of two providers who have waiting lists. Talk with them about why they are successful.
- Update your Facebook page.
- Anticipate how many school-age openings you will have for the summer and tell your CCR&R agency.

May

- Conduct a cleanup project for the outside of your home. Plant flowers in the front yard.
- Set (or raise) your summer rates now so parents have adequate notice. Reevaluate your vacation-pay policy regarding parents who leave in the summer but plan to return in the fall.
- Locate at least three provider websites on the Internet. Write down three marketing ideas you could use.
- Send a thank-you card to current and past clients for Mother's Day.

June

- Update your contract with parents.
- Distribute fifty business flyers at local businesses.
- Send a thank-you card to current and past clients for Father's Day.
- Update your Facebook page.
- Run an ad through one of the many online classified ad services.

July

- Distribute one hundred door hangers in your neighborhood.
- Start a newsletter for parents.
- Conduct a local park cleaning with your children. Send photos and an article to your local newspaper.

August

- Call your CCR&R agency to update your listing and talk to a referral counselor about parent demand.
- Start a photo album showing off your benefits.
- Place a classified ad on Craigslist.

September

- Raise your rates by 4 percent over the next three months.
- Send to the grandparents of your children a card with a photograph for Grandparents Day.
- Update your Facebook page.

October

- Throw a Halloween party and invite the neighborhood children. Distribute your business flyers or business cards to trick-or-treaters.
- Write an article on safe trick-or-treating for your local newspaper. Give copies of your article (written on your business letterhead) to parents and ask them to distribute copies to their friends and coworkers.
- Attend a workshop on child development.

November

- Join the Chamber of Commerce.
- Run another ad through an online classified ad service.

December

- Set up your own website.
- Provide free child care on a Friday evening so families can shop.
- Identify one new benefit you will add to your program for the next year.
- Hold a holiday get-together for your current customers.
- Update your Facebook page.

APPENDIX B

How Much Do You Want to Earn? A Worksheet to Calculate a Weekly Rate for Parents

Use these worksheets to calculate a weekly rate for your services. The first worksheet is for new providers. The second worksheet is for providers who have been in business for at least one full tax year.

A Worksheet for New Providers to Calculate a Weekly Rate for Parents

Use this worksheet if you have been in business for less than one full tax year.

1	Enter the hourly rate goal (salary) you want to earn ($8.00 per hour, $10.50 per hour, and so on).	(1)	_____
2	Enter the number of hours you will work in a year (include the hours when children are present along with working hours when children are not present, such as during cleaning, food preparation, and record keeping.	(2)	_____
3	Multiply line 1 by line 2. This calculates your annual net earnings (salary) goal.	(3)	_____
4	Divide line 3 by 0.63 (63%). This calculates the gross annual income you will need to earn to meet your annual net earnings goal.	(4)	_____
5	Subtract line 3 from line 4. This calculates your estimated annual business expenses.	(5)	_____
6	Enter the number of children you want in your care.	(6)	_____
7	Divide line 4 by line 6. This calculates the annual income per child.	(7)	_____
8	Enter the number of weeks you want to work each year (52 weeks is an entire year).	(8)	_____
9	Divide line 7 by line 8. This calculates the weekly fee you must charge parents to reach your hourly rate goal (line 1).	(9)	_____

A Worksheet for Experienced Providers to Calculate a Weekly Rate for Parents

Use this worksheet if you have been in business for at least one full tax year.

1 Enter the hourly rate goal (salary) you want to earn
   ($8.00 per hour, $10.50 per hour, and so on).   (1) _____

2 Enter the number of hours you work in a year (include
   the hours when children are present along with working
   hours when children are not present, such as during
   cleaning, food preparation, and record keeping). (Use the
   amount on line 4 from your IRS **Form 8829**.)   (2) _____

3 Multiply line 1 by line 2. This calculates your annual
   net earnings (salary) goal.   (3) _____

4 Enter your annual business expenses. (Use the amount
   on line 28 of your IRS **Schedule C**.)   (4) _____

5 Add line 3 to line 4. This calculates the gross annual
   income you will need to earn to meet your annual
   net earnings goal.   (5) _____

6 Enter the number of children you want in your care.   (6) _____

7 Divide line 4 by line 6. This calculates the annual income
   per child.   (7) _____

8 Enter the number of weeks you want to work each year
   (52 weeks is an entire year).   (8) _____

9 Divide line 7 by line 8. This calculates the weekly fee you
   must charge parents to reach your hourly rate goal (line 1).   (9) _____

Parent Call Tracking Form

Date of call   _____

Name of parent(s)   _____

Address   _____

Phone # home _____ work _____ mobile _____

E-mail   _____

Name of child   _____ Birth date _____

                              _____ Birth date _____

                              _____ Birth date _____

Desired start date _____ Rate quoted _____

Any special interests or needs of the child _____

_____

_____

How did you hear about my program?

     ☐ Flyer: where did you pick it up? _____

     ☐ Sign on my lawn

     ☐ Classified ad: name of newspaper   _____

     ☐ Child care resource and referral agency referral

     ☐ Referral from an individual: name   _____

     ☐ Other: identify _____

Parent concerns/notes: _____

_____

Date interview scheduled _____

If parent declined interview, why? _____

If I turned parent down, why? _____

Parent Interview Checklist

Date of interview _____

Name of parent(s) _____

Address _____

Phone # home _____ work _____ mobile _____

E-mail _____

Name of child _____ Birth date _____

_____ Birth date _____

_____ Birth date _____

Desired start date _____ Rate quoted _____

Parent references:

Name _____ Relationship _____ Phone # _____

Name _____ Relationship _____ Phone # _____

Name _____ Relationship _____ Phone # _____

How does the parent show an interest in the child's behavior during the interview?

_____

Does the parent show a willingness to be flexible and adapt to my rules?

Yes ___ No ___ Any problems _____

Signs that the child may be difficult to care for _____

_____

Does the parent treat me with respect and have a positive attitude? Yes _____ No _____

Comments _____

Questions raised by the parent that concern me _____

What do I like about this family? _____

What concerns do I have about this family? _____

Skills Children Learn in Family Child Care

Activity	Specific Skills Learned
Finding toys or learning materials to work with alone or with others	*Cognitive:* Makes decisions about interests and abilities. *Self-help:* Finds toys by himself or sets up environment for play. *Social/language:* Learns to share, barter, manage conflict, and ask for help. *Emotional:* Learns about acceptance and rejection. Expresses needs.
Block play	*Cognitive:* May count blocks and see pattern and design. Learns to build and plan structure. Matches blocks that look alike. *Social:* Learns to share and cooperate. *Physical:* Learns to balance blocks and line them up (small-motor coordination).
Dramatic play	*Cognitive:* Decides appropriate dress and appearance for roles; uses visual perceptions to assess self, others, and play environment. Learns and remembers behaviors to imitate. Develops abstract thinking abilities. *Social:* Plays adult roles. Develops self-image and coordinates with others. Learns to express feelings. *Language:* Learns to express self in another role.
Setting the table	*Cognitive:* Counts silverware, glasses, and napkins, or places one object by each setting. Follows pattern of place settings. Knows which is soup spoon or salad fork. *Social:* Cooperates with other children. May teach younger children to help. *Physical:* Picks up and places objects (small-motor coordination).

Sitting down to eat	*Cognitive:* Measures to pour. Understands directions. *Social/language:* Learns appropriate table conversation and manners. *Physical:* Pours milk, passes dishes (small-motor coordination).
Story time or listening to music	*Cognitive:* Listens and retains information. Follows story line (sequencing) with eyes and/or ears. Recognizes words, pictures, instruments, and rhythms.
Fingerplays and songs	*Cognitive/language:* Learns words, gestures, and melody (sequencing, repetition, speech, and listening skills). Follows directions. *Physical:* Coordination (small and large motor) for gestures and fingerplays.
Dance	*Cognitive/language:* Listens to music and rhythms. Learns to understand simple movement directions and their relationship to the music. *Physical:* Coordinates movements (large motor).
Climbing/riding	*Cognitive:* May count the rungs to the top of a climbing structure; plans climb. Maps out direction and distance to ride; watches for others in path. *Social:* Takes turns, interacts. *Physical:* Large-motor coordination, balance.
Sand play	*Cognitive:* Measures sand and maps out roads (spatial relationships). *Social:* Shares, interacts, cooperates. *Physical:* Pours, dumps, pushes, gathers, scoops, packs (small and large motor).
Putting away toys	*Cognitive:* Sorts toys, follows directions. *Social:* Takes turns, learns to handle toys carefully. *Physical:* Places object on the shelf, replaces lids, opens and shuts doors.

Choosing Child Care Checklist

Choosing Child Care Checklist

Provider _____

Date program was contacted _____

Address _____

_____

Phone number—home _____

Phone number—work _____

Phone number—mobile _____

Ages of children now enrolled, not
including the provider's own children _____

Ages of provider's own children _____

Hours open _____

Cost per hour/week/month

Infant _____

Toddler _____

Preschooler _____

Schoolager _____

Other fees

Enrollment fee _____

Number of yearly paid holidays _____

Number of yearly paid vacation days
taken by parent _____

Other _____

Special services offered _____

_____

_____

Key benefits of the program   _____

_____

_____

Training credentials   _____

_____

References   _____

Top Five Signs of Quality to Look for in a Child Care Program

1 A small group size
2 A program focused on meeting children's needs
3 A safe place for children
4 A program where there are lots of fun things for children to do
5 A provider with training in child development

Enrollment Form

_____ (*parent[s] name*) hereby agree to enroll

their child _____ (*name of child*) with the _____

_____(*name of program*). The first day of enrollment will be

_____ (*date*). Provider promises to begin providing care for this child on

the first day of enrollment.

Parent(s) will pay an enrollment fee of $ _____ that will hold this spot until the

first day of enrollment. This fee is due at the signing of this form. This enrollment fee

is nonrefundable whether or not the parent brings the child for care. Parent will sign

and return the provider's contract on or by the first day of care.

_____   _____

Parent signature   Date of signature

_____   _____

Parent signature   Date of signature

_____   _____

Parent signature   Date of signature

Waiting List Form

1 Name of parent(s) _____

Address _____

Phone # home _____ work _____ mobile _____

E-mail _____ Date placed on waiting list _____

Name of child(ren) _____ Birth date _____

_____ Birth date _____

_____ Birth date _____

Desired start date _____ Rate quoted _____

Notes _____

_____

2 Name of parent(s) _____

Address _____

Phone # home _____ work _____ mobile _____

E-mail _____ Date placed on waiting list _____

Name of child(ren) _____ Birth date _____

_____ Birth date _____

_____ Birth date _____

Desired start date _____ Rate quoted _____

Notes _____

_____

3 Name of parent(s) _____

Address _____

Phone # home _____ work _____ mobile _____

E-mail _____ Date placed on waiting list _____

Name of child(ren) _____ Birth date _____

_____ Birth date _____

_____ Birth date _____

Desired start date _____ Rate quoted _____

Notes _____

_____

4 Name of parent(s) _____

Address _____

Phone # home _____ work _____ mobile _____

E-mail _____ Date placed on waiting list _____

Name of child(ren) _____ Birth date _____

_____ Birth date _____

_____ Birth date _____

Desired start date _____ Rate quoted _____

Notes _____

_____

5 Name of parent(s) _____

Address _____

Phone # home _____ work _____ mobile _____

E-mail _____ Date placed on waiting list _____

Name of child(ren) _____ Birth date _____

_____ Birth date _____

_____ Birth date _____

Desired start date _____ Rate quoted _____

Notes _____

_____

6 Name of parent(s) _____

Address _____

Phone # home _____ work _____ mobile _____

E-mail _____ Date placed on waiting list _____

Name of child(ren) _____ Birth date _____

_____ Birth date _____

_____ Birth date _____

Desired start date _____ Rate quoted _____

Notes _____

_____

Sample Press Release

PRESS RELEASE
FOR IMMEDIATE RELEASE
DECEMBER 28, 20xx

FOR MORE INFORMATION CONTACT:
OWNER LI'L DARLINGS, XXX-XXXX
LOCAL CHILD CARE PROVIDER FEATURED IN GRAND AVENUE PARADE

This year the annual Grand Avenue New Year's Day Parade will feature children from the Li'l Darlings Family Child Care Home. The five children from the four families enrolled in this child care program will be dressed in handmade costumes matching the parade's theme, "From the Frontier to the New Age."

Roberta Darling, the owner of Li'l Darlings, says she wanted her children to participate in the parade because it will be a fun activity for them. "They have worked very hard over the past two months to plan their costumes and decorate the wagons they will be pulling," Darling says. Darling's program was chosen as one of the three new parade participants selected each year by the parade committee.

Li'l Darlings is a licensed family child care program that has been in operation for three years. It is located on Portland Avenue near Laurel Street. Li'l Darlings serves children from ages six weeks to six years. Roberta Darling recently earned her early childhood development degree from Concordia College.

###

Parent Evaluation Form

1 Overall, how would you rate the care I provide your child? Circle one.

Needs Improvement   *Pretty Good*   *Wonderful*

   1   2   3   4

2 What do you like best about my program?

   _____

   _____

3 What could I do to improve my program?

   _____

   _____

4 Would you recommend my program to other parents? Why or why not?

   _____

   _____

5 Would you like to volunteer in my program? Doing what?

   _____

   _____

6 How could I advertise my program to attract new clients?

   _____

   _____

7 What additional "special services" are you interested in that I could offer?

   _____

   _____

8 Other comments or suggestions:

   _____

   _____

Parent's name (optional) _____ Date _____

Child's name (optional) _____

Photo, Voice, Website, Facebook, and Video Permission Form

Waiver and Release

I/we hereby consent to the use of the voice or the likeness in photographs, audio, or on videotape of _____ (*name of child*) by the _____ (*name of child care program*) in the production of any business flyers, newsletters, websites, voice mail messages, videotapes, and any other advertisements or promotions that _____ _____ (*name of child care program*) may decide to develop, now or in the future.

In addition, I/we hereby consent to the use of the voice or likeness in photographs or on videotape of _____ (*name of child*) by the _____ (*name of child care program*) to be posted on my Facebook/MySpace page. [Note: this permission could be limited to one or a few photos, rather than this general permission.]

I/we also hereby agree to waive and forgo any right or entitlement of claim I/we might have to any compensation, fees, or other benefits except for a waiver fee of $1.00.

Further, by signing this waiver and release, I/we certify that I/we am/are the legal parent or guardian of the child identified above.

Parent/Guardian _____

Parent/Guardian _____

Date _____

Tax Benefits of Becoming a Regulated Family Child Care Provider

	Unregulated or Illegal Provider	Regulated or "Exempt" Provider	Regulated and Food Program	Fill in Your Estimate
Income				
Parent fees				
(4 children x $160 per week)	$33,280	$33,280	$33,280	_____
Food Program—Tier II				
($205/month for 4 children)	$0	$0	$2,460	_____
Total Income	$33,280	$33,280	$35,740	_____
Business Deductions				
Advertising	$400	$400	$400	_____
Business interest	$80	$80	$80	_____
Office expense	$1,750	$1,750	$1,750	_____
Supplies	$2,000	$2,000	$2,000	_____
Laundry/cleaning	$150	$150	$150	_____
Food	$5,000	$5,000	$5,000	_____
Dues, books	$200	$200	$200	_____
Training expenses	$200	$200	$200	_____
Household items	$700	$700	$700	_____
Toys	$500	$500	$500	_____
Car expenses	$750	$750	$750	_____
Depreciation on $8,000 of				
appliances and furniture	$400	$400	$400	_____
Utilities ($700 x 35% T/S†)	*	$245	$245	_____
House depreciation				
($162,000 home x 35% T/S† over 39 yrs)	*	$1,450	$1,450	_____
Homeowner's insurance				
($800 x 35% T/S†)	*	$280	$280	_____
Mortgage interest ($3,000 x 35% T/S†)	*	$1,050	$1,050	_____
Property taxes ($1,600 x 35% T/S†)	*	$560	$560	_____
Total Deductions	$12,130	$15,715	$15,715	_____
Taxable Income				
(Income—Deductions)	$21,150	$17,565	$20,025	_____

Social Security Tax (13.65%)	$2,887	$2,398	$2,733	_____
Federal Income Tax(15%)	$3,173	$2,635	$3,004	_____
Gross Profit (Taxable Income—Taxes)	$15,090	$12,532	$14,288	_____
House expenses (marked above with an *) that are not deductible	$-3,585	-0	-0	_____
Net Profit (Gross Profit— House expenses not allowed)	**$11,505**	**$12,532**	**$14,288**	_____

†T/S means Time-Space percentage. See the *Family Child Care Record-Keeping Guide,* 8th edition, for more information.

*These are not deductible for unregulated providers.

It is a federal law that child care providers earning money by caring for children in their home (whether licensed, regulated, exempt from regulation, or illegal) must report their income to the IRS. Many providers do not report their income, either because they aren't aware of the tax laws or because they are worried that they will owe too much in taxes. This appendix is designed to show how all providers can significantly reduce their taxes. For federal tax purposes, a child care provider falls into one of two categories:

1   A provider who is required to meet but does not meet state regulations (such as licensing or registration) is called an unregulated or illegal provider. Although the author does not recommend being unregulated, such providers should be aware that they can take many business tax deductions if they report their income. See column one of the chart. Taking deductions can greatly reduce any taxes owed.

2   A provider who does meet state regulations is called a regulated provider. A regulated provider is entitled to claim house expenses (house depreciation, insurance, mortgage interest, property taxes, and utilities) that an unregulated provider cannot claim. A provider who is exempt from state regulations is entitled to all the same deductions as a regulated provider but is usually not eligible to participate in the Food Program. Regulated providers can increase their net profit by joining the Food Program.

Besides claiming additional tax deductions, there are many other benefits of becoming a regulated child care provider:

- Join the Food Program and be reimbursed for some of your food expenses.
- Obtain liability insurance to protect your business.
- Join a local association of family child care providers and receive the benefits of membership.
- Sign up to be listed by your local child care resource and referral agency, which will refer parents to your business.
- Attend training workshops and receive other support services.
- Become eligible for local grant and loan programs in some areas.

Notes on the chart: The numbers in the chart are only estimates shown for comparison purposes. Your income and expenses will vary. Not all the business deductions or tax consequences are shown on this chart. We used a 35% Time/Space percentage (T/S) representing the portion of the home used for business. We used a 15% federal income tax rate. Notice that the deductions are the same for each provider, except that the unregulated provider cannot claim expenses associated with the house. By losing these deductions, this provider pays more taxes. These deductions (totaling $3,585) are subtracted from the unregulated provider's gross income because the provider had to pay these expenses anyway, even though they are not allowed as a business deduction. Also notice that an exempt provider (one who is not required to meet local regulations) can claim all of the same deductions as a regulated provider. The provider on the Food Program pays more taxes but has the highest net profit. Every provider is better off by joining the Food Program.

Additional Resources

Organizations

Center for the Child Care Workforce
555 New Jersey Avenue NW
Washington, DC 20001
202-662-8005
www.ccw.org
Original sponsor of the Worthy Wage Campaign and Worthy Wage Day (May 1).
Publications on wages and working conditions and information about Quality Rating
and Improvement Systems (QRIS).

Council for Professional Recognition
2460 Sixteenth Street NW
Washington, DC 20009
800-424-4310
www.cdacouncil.org
Information about the Child Development Associate (CDA) credential.

Monday Morning America, Inc.
Monday Morning Moms: A Family Day Care Management Service Franchise
908-668-6840
www.mondayam.com
A family child care provider management service.

National Association for Family Child Care
1743 West Alexander Street
Salt Lake City, UT 84119
801-866-2322
www.nafcc.org
Information about local associations, newsletters, and accreditation programs. Also
has a variety of publications, including "Why Choose Nationally Accredited Family
Child Care?" brochure: www.qualitycareforchildren.org/files/NAFCC_Accreditation_
Brochuer.pdf.

National Association for the Education of Young Children
1313 L Street, NW, Suite 500
Washington, DC 20005
800-424-2460
www.naeyc.org
Membership information, publications, and training.

National Association of Child Care Resource and Referral Agencies
1515 North Courthouse Road, 11th Floor
Arlington, VA 22201
703-341-4100
www.naccrra.org
Information about how to contact your local CCR&R agency and publications.

Provider Appreciation Day
National Association of Child Care Resource and Referral Agencies
703-341-4115
www.providerappreciationday.org
An annual day of appreciation for all child care providers celebrated the Friday before Mother's Day.

Quality Rating and Improvement System (QRIS)
The QRIS National Learning Network (http://qrisnetwork.org) is a clearing house of information about state programs. For a list of state QRIS contacts: http://qrisnetwork .org/state-qris-contacts.

Redleaf Press
800-423-8309
www.redleafpress.org
The Go Green Rating Scale for Early Childhood Settings
The Go Green Rating Scale for Early Childhood Settings Handbook
Family Child Care Curriculum
Redleaf Press offers exceptional resources for early childhood professionals, including a complete line of books and other materials specifically created for family child care providers.